Executives in Action

A Guide to Balanced Decision-making
in Management

Executives in Action

A Guide to Balanced Decision-making in Management

Carol-Lynne Moore

MACDONALD AND EVANS

MACDONALD & EVANS LTD
Estover, Plymouth PL6 7PZ

First published as *Action Profiling* 1978
Second edition published as *Executives in Action* 1982
Reprinted 1984

Printed in Great Britain by
Hollen Street Press Ltd, Slough
Phototypeset by *Sunrise Setting*, Torquay, Devon

Preface

Senior management is a balancing act, a tightrope walk between success and failure. How well a senior manager can perform on this high wire, how sure his footing is, how clever his timing, how acute his judgment — these things not only determine the course of his career, but also critically affect the life of his company. In senior management the risks are high and the mis-steps often fatal.

The metaphor used here is one of movement, chosen for a reason. The very word "manage" comes from a word involving movement, the Latin word "manidiare" meaning "to handle", and the origin of the word provides insight into the tightrope act of today's executive. To manage implies a kind of "hands on" control, grappling with problems, shaping plans, seizing opportunities. Management is the hand of man in action, both literally and metaphorically.

Over the past 30 years management consultant Warren Lamb has been studying managers in action. He has discovered that, just as one can think in words or in images, so too one can think in movement. And this is just what managers do, every time they make a decision. Lamb has developed a tool called the Action Profile to help managers understand movement thinking better and use it to stay on top of the balancing act.

No two managers walk the tightrope of decision-making in exactly the same way. The point of balance, the subtlety of coordination, the sequence of steps differ for each manager. The Action Profile makes it possible to understand and appreciate the distinctive styles of senior managers, and from this understanding all kinds of new managerial feats become possible.

When Action Profiling was created by Warren Lamb 30 years ago, it was ahead of its time. Now, as we move towards the twenty-first century, the ancient concept of movement being central both to thinking and to acting is being confirmed by contemporary research. We now know that movement behaviour forms a large component of all human communication. Movement has meaning and through disciplined perception, like that upon which the Action Profile is founded, one can learn to understand the meaning of movement better. How this understanding can be applied to improve decision-making in senior management is the subject of this book.

AUTHOR'S NOTE

One of the difficulties of writing is accurately matching language with the idea one is attempting to convey. In my case it is the pronouns which have caused me trouble.

Action Profiles have now been drawn for over 10,000 men and women. On the basis of this data there is not a single trait found more commonly in one sex than the other. Decision-making style does not appear to be determined in any way by gender.

In Chapters 2 and 11 of this book, various aspects of decision-making are described in general terms rather than by reference to specific individuals. Because I did not wish to exclude, by implication, either men or women from these discussions, I experimented with various pronoun blends (he/she, s/he, him/her, etc.). Unfortunately, I found that accurate usage made for very awkward reading.

Consequently, masculine pronoun forms are used in all general discussions to represent both men and women. Elsewhere, in specific case histories, pronouns correspond with the gender of the individual described. These specific case histories, both of individuals and of companies, are factual, although obvious identifying features (such as names, products, etc.) have been changed to respect the confidentiality of those described.

ACKNOWLEDGMENTS

Many thanks to my mentors Warren Lamb and Pamela Ramsden for their tireless advice and generous assistance in the preparation of this book. Many thanks also to those companies who made reports available for publication; to my friends and colleagues who appear in the photographs; to Marjorie Waxman for her help with the design; and to Daniel Nagrin for his supportive criticism.

The photographs were taken by the author.

Action Profile is the trade mark of Warren Lamb Associates.

1982   CLM

Contents

PART 3 TOP TEAM PLANNING — THE PROFILE IN ACTION AND INTERACTION

PART ONE
Individual Decision-Making Style

CHAPTER 1

Three Fables for Managers

THE LADY OR THE TIGER?

Mr Carey was worried. In two hours he had to make his recommendation to the chief executive for the appointment of a new marketing director. It was an important appointment, and a difficult choice. Whom would he choose?

Files of the two shortlisted candidates lay on his desk. They seemed to stare at him like two blank doors. Mr Carey tried to imagine who waited behind those doors; a snarling tiger who could wreck the company, an innovative marketing whizz-kid, a ... .

Mr Carey shook himself. For a moment he had felt like the poor fellow in the story who was condemned by the king to open one of two doors. Behind one, a ferocious tiger who would eat him for lunch. Behind the other, a gorgeous princess who would marry him. "Over-dramatising again, Carey," he chided himself. "This is not a life or death decision. There are two qualified candidates; one, surely, will do."

He opened the file on the left, that of Chester Rawlings. Chester Rawlings was a wiry man in his early forties. He gave Mr Carey the impression of someone for ever crouched on the starting line of a race, waiting for the crack of the pistol. He seemed ready to bolt into action at any moment, and his track record *was* impressive. Rawlings had started as a salesman and worked his way up to regional sales manager. He was efficient, well-organised and he could get results, especially when he knew the terrain and someone else had laid the groundwork.

That was what bothered Mr Carey about Rawlings. Company strategy called for developing new products and marketing areas. Did Rawlings have enough imagination? Was he really a pioneer, able to adapt to a new situation? Carey wondered.

In the interview, Carey had sensed a diffident independence in Rawlings. Did Rawlings have a chip on his shoulder? Since his region was organised as a profit centre he had been able to function autonomously up till now. Could he function as well as a member of the senior team, or was he too much a loner? Carey sighed, closing the folder, and flipped open its companion file.

Paulette Westbrook was another story. Westbrook was an alert, enthusiastic woman in her mid-forties. A dynamic leader with a reputation for being a good listener, she had welded their market research department into a tightly-knit team. No need to worry about her fitting into a group; Westbrook could work with anyone.

Carey knew that, as a market research person, Westbrook was superb. She was thorough and careful. She had shown the persistence and creativity necessary to pioneer the company's marketing strategy. On the other hand, if you placed Westbrook directly in the line of fire, would she respond decisively and quickly enough? Could she keep pace with the market trends? Or would she let opportunities slip by while she finished her research?

Carey closed the file, fidgeting. He thought he knew what the company needed. He'd studied the candidates' records, interviewed both individuals thoroughly. Why were these major appointments always so difficult? The folders seemed to glare at him inscrutably. They did look like closed doors. Who was the lady? Who was the tiger? Who was really inside the file? The chief executive was waiting. Carey picked up the files. You never know the validity of your choice until you actually make the appointment. And then, he mused reaching for the door knob, it's always too late ....

ICARUS

Fred Berne was successful. Not only was he good at his job, he liked it. He made a good salary, he was well-liked by his colleagues, and the job itself stimulated him.

Berne handled internal sales administration for a clothes merchandising firm. The major decisions were up to someone else; he just kept things running smoothly. Whether it was making salesmen's travel arrangements, making sure deliveries were made on time, or keeping tabs on the cost of maintaining their stock, Berne was a thorough, far-sighted and capable administrator.

Naturally, with this good performance, Berne came up for promotion. Although he wasn't sure he wanted the position, the added prestige and increased salary were irresistible, and Berne became chief buyer for the chain.

With his pockets full of money he flew to New York to choose the winter line. While he knew everything about the merchandise the stores had been carrying, he had never been responsible for choosing their lines and had never been exposed to what the market as a whole had to offer. With so many choices in front of him, Berne felt he needed a month to make up his mind. Instead, he had a week. The speed with which he had to make decisions and the responsibility panicked him. He chose, but he chose badly. His mistakes cost the company a lot of money, as well as costing him his job.

"I was a victim of the Peter Principle," he moaned. "I simply failed in the new job. I flew too high, and when I fell, it was bloody. If I hadn't taken the promotion, I'd still be working for that company. I'd be the highest paid junior executive in town. And I'd still be happy."

THE MAN WHO CRIED WOLF

Ernest Dobson was the financial officer for a small entrepreneurial firm producing furniture and house-wares. The firm had been started by an Italian artist after his furniture designs began to sell. Creative and impetuous, the artist had gathered other designers around him. The team he created had generated a number of successful designs and had expanded their product line rapidly. Gradually they were acquiring a professional administrative staff to keep the business running, but at the time that Dobson joined the firm the designers themselves were still making all the major company decisions. Dobson was the only professional manager on the senior team, and he was unhappy. He felt himself to be the odd man out, firstly because he was a businessman and not an artist, and secondly because he could never seem to fit in with the style generated by the others.

The artist-owner had collected a senior team which in many ways was a replica of his own temperament. This gave an impetuous, wildly exploratory bent to the whole company. Dobson complained privately that he never knew what their product line was. "One month we're into silverware," he said, "and the next we're buying a plastics plant."

Dobson himself was resolute, down-to-earth, practical and thorough. He hated being rushed into things and he loathed the fact that there was no consistency to company policy. In fact, as far as he could tell, there was no company policy at all, just hundreds of wild ideas. Maybe he wasn't creative, but he could accurately evaluate the viability of an idea from a business point of view, and financially he knew what he was talking about. The longer he was with the company, the more convinced he became that they were expanding too rapidly.

"Financially we're in a dangerous position," he explained in numerous meetings. He was adamant, he was clear, he was persuasive, he was provocative, yet he could not rally any support for his point of view. He couldn't even get his colleagues to engage in debate with him.

"I felt like the boy who cried wolf," Dobson bitterly recalled after the company nearly went bankrupt. "It was as if I stood on a soapbox, haranguing deaf people, while the company drifted nearer and nearer financial disaster. There was nothing I could do without cooperation from the others. For some reason we just weren't on the same wavelength. My contributions were never accepted."

THE MORAL

These three fables illustrate three problems that are neither unknown nor uncommon in executive teams. In *The Lady or the Tiger* the puzzle is to match the suitable appointee with his job and with the team in which he will operate. In *Icarus* the problem is to avoid promoting an individual to a job for which he is not suited, while in *The Man Who Cried Wolf* the crux is to ensure that the expertise of an individual is not lost because of a communication breakdown.

Each of these fables underlines the fact that effective

management is more than just training and skill. These stories point out that there are other potent, if intangible, factors which influence the effectiveness of an executive's performance. These mysterious factors are sometimes called "style".

Managers have style and so do companies. Sometimes these styles are complementary, and sometimes, as in the case of Mr Dobson and the design company, they clash. Matching personal styles and company styles for maximum compatibility and efficacy is a personnel director's headache, as Mr Carey could assure us. And sometimes, as with poor Fred Berne, a winning style in one position is a losing style in another.

In short, style plays a role in all executive actions and interactions. But what is style?

CHAPTER 2

What's in a Style?

Style can be defined as the way in which something is done. As a word, style comes from the Latin root *stylus*, which denoted a writing instrument. If we couple this meaning with our contemporary definition, we can say that style is the manner and means by which action is

Decision-making style is the manner and means by which action is executed.

executed. Management style, then, is *how an individual goes about making a decision*. Style is manner, not matter.

For example, three senior managers of a small firm may all arrive at the same conclusion. They may all decide that the company should launch a new product. But how these individuals arrive at this decision may differ radically. The marketing director may have made the decision impetuously, with an eye to beating the competition. The finance director may have made the decision deliberately, by carefully researching the product and plotting out details in advance. The managing director may have arrived at his decision through the conviction that the product was valuable and necessary and therefore ought to be made. In this example the decision of each executive is the same — launch the product — but the manner and means by which each person drew his conclusions are quite different.

At this point one is tempted to ask "Why does it matter how they arrive at their conclusions, as long as they agree and the product shows a profit? Doesn't style belong more to the realm of aesthetics than to the province of management?" Certainly, the emphasis in managerial decision-making must be on results. However, while we can separate the style of decision-making from the content of the decision for purposes of analysis, in actual management practice the two are integrally wedded, so much so that the style of the decision-makers can actually alter the impact of the decision.

Decision-making style, for example, can have deleterious effects. A product can be launched with too little preparation, without adequate research or testing. A decision can be made so slowly that a marketing lead is lost to competitors. A resolution to see through product development can be maintained tenaciously when new discoveries and a market pressure indicate that the plan really should be abandoned.

Style can turn a modest decision into a wildly successful venture.

On the other hand style can turn a modest decision into a wildly successful venture. For example, prompt aggressive commitment can help a company stay ahead of its competitors. Careful cautious decision-making may delay execution but can vouchsafe quality and long-term profits. Firm conviction on the part of executives can guarantee that the company will see through the development of a much-needed product in spite of external or internal delays.

THE THREE STAGES OF DECISION-MAKING

To better understand this complex relationship of style and action, it is helpful to visualise decision-making as a three-stage process. These stages will be described first in terms of the *action* that takes place and then in terms of the *style* or manner in which the action is taken.

The first stage in decision-making involves getting oriented to the problem which is to be solved. Probing, ferreting out information, defining and categorising facts, questioning old assumptions, seeking alternatives and correlating new data with old, these are all activities which take place in the first stage of the decision-making process. This stage is called the *attention* phase, and includes the preliminary research and survey necessary before a decision can be made.

Once a manager has done some homework he passes into what is called the *intention* stage. In this stage a course of action must be determined. Possible projects and decisions are evaluated with an eye to immediate needs and company policy. The purpose of the proposed action is clarified and a firm resolution upon a course of action is forged. Unless the resolution to act is established and supported by the conviction that the proposed action is important, interest fades and there will be no action. Thus, the intention stage is the critical bridge between preliminary consideration and actual execution.

Convinced he is on the right track, the executive then proceeds to implement the decision. This is the *commitment* stage. The decision agreed on must be accurately paced and the consequences of the action anticipated. This involves acting at the appropriate moment, keeping tabs on developments, and being able to update and reschedule implementation as the project proceeds.

The commitment stage is the part of the process where the most risks are taken. Once the project is in motion, it is often difficult or impossible to slow the wheels or reverse the direction. It is in the commitment phase that managerial blunders most often come to light. This may be the reason why managers are so preoccupied with this particular stage of the action process. Commitment *is* critical, but so are gathering information and sifting out issues and priorities. Every manager attends, intends and commits on the job, yet he goes about these activities in a highly individual *manner*. This is the essence of style. What can we discern about management style relative to each stage of the action process?

THE HOW OF ATTENDING

If we ask how an individual behaves when "attending", we can distinguish two different yet complementary approaches.

An executive may approach the obtaining of information in an *investigative* manner. This manager's appetite for information is intense. He is analytical, penetrating, thorough and cautious. A stickler for details, he is meticulous about preliminary research. As a result, he may be a bit of a fuss-budget for whom categorising facts and checking accuracy become ends in themselves. Yet it is this proclivity for amassing detailed information that is the forte of the investigative manager.

Another manager will approach the attention stage in an *exploratory* manner. This individual manifests a radar-like attentiveness. He needs to survey as broad a range of information as possible. Always on the lookout for alternatives, he can be creative, inventive, iconoclastic. This wide-ranging view can lead the explorer to be scatter-brained and a bit too easily beguiled by the greener grass on the other side of the hill, yet when it comes to seeing analogies between existing facts and appreciating research from several fields, the exploratory executive is a whizz-kid.

THE HOW OF INTENDING

We can discern two different, yet complementary, approaches to forming an intention.

An executive may go about this process in a *determined* way. This manager will build up a case to support his view of a proposed action and once resolved, he will not be thrown off track by a gnat's eyelash or even by an elephant. The greater the challenge, the more this bulldog is ready to sink his teeth in and stand his ground. Such conviction can lead to stubborn inflexible behaviour, yet when it comes to persisting against difficult odds the determined executive is the one for the job.

Another manager may arrive at an intention in an *evaluative*[1] manner. This individual forms convictions by sizing up a proposal. His style is critical, challenging, provocative. He is always inflating and deflating issues in order to establish what is most important. Because an evaluator sees only black and white, he may over-simplify a situation, but when it comes to clarifying priorities, to discerning the important projects from the trivial and unrealistic, depend on the evaluative executive.

THE HOW OF COMMITTING

There are also two different, yet complementary, ways to handle the implementation of a project.

---

1. This manner of forming an intention was formerly termed *confronting*. The term was recently changed to *evaluating* by Pamela Ramsden to describe this decision-making style more accurately.

Some managers handle implementation through judicious awareness of *timing*[1]. This managerial type tends to be impatient with lengthy research and long debates on policy. The closer a project is to the "doing" stage, the better he likes it. The time-keeper will have an eye open for opportunities and will be ready to act competitively if need be. This need to respond without delay means that he can act thoughtlessly and rashly. To some extent, the time-keeping manager matches our view of the "go-getter". He knows the opportune moment for action and is ready to make a quick start to beat the crowd.

A different style of making a commitment is seen in the *anticipatory* manager. This individual's approach to implementation is to stay one step ahead of what is actually taking place. He keeps tabs on developments and plots out results in advance. This person does not like to be surprised by unexpected events and is seldom caught off his guard. However, by wanting to work things out too early, he may foresee problems that do not exist. Still, count on the upbeat anticipator to evaluate the practical aspects of implementing a project and to sense trends and future developments.

THE SIX BASIC MANAGEMENT STYLES

Using the three-stage action process of attention–intention–commitment, we can depict six basic management styles. The following chart briefly outlines these.

---

1. This manner of handling commitment was formerly called *deciding*. The term was recently changed to *timing* by Pamela Ramsden to describe this decision-making style more accurately.

Attention stage	
Investigative style	*Exploratory style*
Probing, scanning and classifying information within a prescribed area. Outcome: systematic research, establishing methods and defining standards.	Broadening scope, uncovering, encompassing and perceiving information from many areas. Outcome: creative brain-storming, discovering alternatives.

Intention stage	
Determined style	*Evaluative style*
Affirming purpose, building resolve, forging conviction, justifying intent. Outcome: persisting against odds, maintaining strength of will.	Gauging pros and cons, sizing up the issues, perceiving proportion. Outcome: clarifying intentions, realistically appraising facts and proposals.

Commitment stage	
Time-keeping	*Anticipatory style*
Pacing implementation, sensing the moment-by-moment timing of action. Outcome: adjusting time priorities for opportune implementation.	Perceiving the developing stages of action and sensing the consequences of each stage. Outcome: setting goals, measuring progress and updating plans.

The three styles listed in the lefthand column above have to do with the exertion of particular kinds of mental and physical energies. Managers with strong invest-igative, determined or time-keeping styles work through focusing, pushing and pacing their actions to make things happen. They are assertive, making their decisions work through the use of "elbow grease" and applied effort.

On the other hand the three styles listed in the righthand column are concerned with relating decisions to each other or to the whole. Managers with strong exploratory, evaluative or anticipatory styles are concerned with getting perspective on their decisions. They are less assertive than investigators, determiners and time-keepers. They design their decisions to achieve the desired results rather than "pushing" for action.

Of course, each assertive style complements a more perspective-oriented style, and vice versa. A manager who is purely investigative is likely to suffer from tunnel vision or from the ills of over-specialisation. An executive who is highly exploratory may make creative leaps which he is unable to substantiate with hard facts. The investigator needs the scope of the explorer, the explorer the depth of the investigator.

Similarly, a determined style and an evaluative style are complementary. A determined manager can become stubborn over an unimportant issue, while an evaluative executive can be clear about the importance of a matter but under pressure may lack the guts to stick with his appraisals. The determiner needs the clarity of the evaluator or his persistence gets out of proportion. The evaluator needs the persistence of the determiner or his assessments lack conviction.

In the commitment stage an assertive time-keeping style complements the more designing anticipatory style. A time-keeping executive can make commitment after commitment but with no sense of where these actions are leading. An anticipatory manager can have a brilliant strategic plan that he bungles through inept timing of the intermediate stages of execution. The time-keeper needs the foresight of the anticipator, while the anticipator needs the sensitive pacing of the time-keeper.

ADAPTABILITY

A factor which affects decision-making style in general is adaptability. Adaptability is the readiness of an individual to change his most basic attitudes to fit an altered situation. Adaptability is closely related to the sequence of attention, intention and commitment in the chain of decision-making. The adaptable manager is motivated to follow this sequence in a stepwise manner — faced with a new situation he first takes time to become informed, then he weighs the pros and cons of the considered action, and finally he acts. In other words the adaptable manager devotes more time and energy to attending and intending that he does to committing. This thorough preliminary work helps to guarantee that he does not make assumptions about the situation which would lead to unsuitable actions. The adaptable manager is actually motivated to adapt his style of management to fit the situation.

The manager who prefers to organise his decision-making in reversed steps, i.e. devoting more time and energy to making commitments than to attending or intending, is likely to be less adaptable. This individual will pass the point of no return on a decision before he has really done his preliminary homework. Placed in a new situation he is likely to assume it to be identical to previously encountered situations and apply procedures which have produced good results in the past. If the situation is the same he will get results remarkably quickly, but if the situation is vastly different from those he has encountered previously his decisions and procedures may be inadequate or inappropriate. The unadaptable manager will attempt to change the situation rather than alter his preferred style of working.

Adaptability in decision-making assures that change will be tolerated within a company, and it helps to ensure that the senior executives do not adhere rigidly to methods which, in a changing world, have become outmoded.

IDENTIFYING

Another general feature of decision-making is called identifying. Identifying can be thought of as an executive's "response quotient" — it is the level of sensitivity to the stimulation provided by his environment. When a manager is highly responsive, he is easily attracted to (or distracted by) the activities of others. Such an individual is spontaneous, enthusiastic, ready to become involved. Executive action sets up vibrations in a company, like ripples across a pond into which a stone has been tossed. The high identifier will want to be as close to the stone as possible. He will personally identify himself with centres of action in the company and will almost automatically want to be included.

A manager who is moderate in identifying will merely respond less spontaneously to the ripples in the pond. The "vibrations" of the work-place will matter less, and the activities of others will be less attractive or distracting to him than they are to the strong identifier.

The centre of action of a company will hold little automatic attraction for the low identifier. This person will be unresponsive to the activities of others, it will be harder to involve him or to arouse his enthusiasm, and he will tend to be aloof, distant and detached from the ripples of action around him.

The level of identifying as a stylistic trait points out an important fact about style. There are times and places when each level of identification is appropriate or inappropriate. In a small entrepreneurial enterprise a high level of identification may be an asset, creating

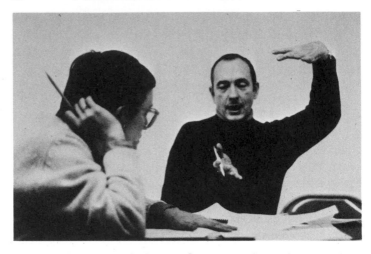

Context determines whether a style is appropriate or inappropriate.

enthusiasm and promoting cohesion in the management team. On the other hand the detachment of the low identifier can be an asset during a crisis.

The same is true of any of the other styles. There are times when being investigative, exploratory, determined, evaluative, aware of timing, or anticipatory is appropriate. There are other times when any one of these styles would be out of place. There is nothing inherently good or bad about any of these decision-making styles. *Context determines whether a style is appropriate or inappropriate.*

We have now described and defined eight elements of managerial style. In the following chapter we will discuss how these different styles are seen in the behaviour of individual managers.

CHAPTER 3

Beyond the Type: The Action Profile

In order to introduce the terminology of management style we have greatly oversimplified it. There is no manager alive whose behaviour corresponds to one of these "pure" types. Every manager, to be effective, must attend, intend and commit. However, management consultant Warren Lamb has found that an executive will apportion his time and energy according to his preferences. A technique called Action Profiling has been developed by Lamb and his colleague Pamela Ramsden. This technique can be used to discern the following aspects of style: which stages of the decision-making process an executive prefers; whether he takes a more assertive or perspective-oriented approach; how adaptable he is; and how intense his need to identify is.

Lamb and Ramsden have discovered that senior managers, who have great latitude of action, will actually restyle their jobs to suit their personal action preferences. For example, an attention-oriented executive will define his role as that of information-gatherer and researcher. An intention-oriented manager will focus on policy-making and difficult projects which test his convictions. The commitment-oriented executive will find a way to put himself where the action is swift-paced and the competition stiff.

In some cases a manager's preferences will be contrary to the actual job description of his position.

What he does may be very different from what he is supposed to do and even from what he claims to be doing. Most professional managers have been trained to use intellectual techniques for making decisions, yet managerial decisions are not always made according to the book, the company policy or even the rules of logic. In actual practice there are irrational factors which often appear to influence decision-making more strongly than logic or training. These factors appear to be irrational simply because, before the development of the Action Profile, we lacked the means to understand style and its effects.

Now Action Profiling makes it possible to be aware of an individual's decision-making style. The Profile can show whether an individual is precise, impetuous, stubborn, provocative, progressive, creative, enthusiastic, etc. Recognising these traits as attributes of the decision-making process removes them from the chaotic, disorderly and emotionally-charged realm of the irrational. Action Profiling makes it possible for an individual to understand his decision-making style and to use this understanding in developing an effective work strategy and in improving relationships with colleagues.

INDIVIDUAL ACTION PROFILES

The Action Profiles and reports which follow are drawn for actual senior managers (the names used here are fictitious). The reports are meant to be used by the individuals themselves following interview and counselling sessions with an Action Profile consultant.

The percentages shown in the Action Profiles represent the relative amount of time and energy which the individual allots to that aspect of decision-making. The more general traits of adaptability and identifying are represented as strong, moderate or low. The reports describe the potential strengths and weaknesses of each aspect of the Profile. Possible actions are discussed and developed by the client and the consultant and are always related to the demands of the actual job.

ATTENTION	Investigating	23%
	Exploring	
		6%
INTENTION	Determining	6%
	Evaluating	22%
COMMITMENT	Timing	29%
	Anticipating	14%

Action Profile of Mr J. F. Gary. Adaptability moderate, identifying moderate.

MR J. F. GARY

Mr J. F. Gary is the chief executive of a medium-sized company which manufactures industrial goods. The company is one of several European subsidiaries of an American company and is organised as a profit centre.

At the time this Profile was drawn Mr Gary had been in his job less than six months. The Profile had two purposes: to help him to know his own strengths and weaknesses in relation to the new job; and to make clear what help and support the head of the European group could provide for him.

ACTION PROFILE REPORT

1.1 Commitment highest, at 43 per cent, with attention and intention roughly equal at 29 per cent and 28 per cent respectively.

Potential strength
You time your activities to achieve results and you measure progress in terms of visible achievements. You are likely to have a reputation for maintaining a results-

oriented and progressive outlook. You can be flexible in your approach to reaching your objectives.

Potential weakness
Realise that you may want to seize opportunities without taking enough time to look for better alternatives or long-term consequences. You may also be discouraged if results do not come as easily as you anticipated.

Possible action
1. Take time to consider alternatives and consequences before committing yourself to an action.
2. Rely on others higher than yourself in exploring and anticipating and ask them such questions as "Can you see a better alternative?" "Can you see any pitfalls if we use this approach?"

1.2   High investigating (23 per cent) combined with low exploring (6 per cent).

Potential strength
You apply a precise, detailed, analytical mind both to seeking information and to processing it. Your methods of operation are likely to be sound and traditional, and therefore you will know what results to expect and will have a background of information with which to compare present results. You are not easily distracted from focusing your attention on a particular matter.

Potential weakness
You are not inclined, on your own initiative, to look for innovative approaches, alternative ways or new ideas. Realise that you may create an environment where such things are actually discouraged.

Possible action
1. Look to others on your staff for innovations, alternatives and new ideas.

2. Attempt to encourage and exploit creative talent in your colleagues and staff, wherever you find it.

1.3 Low determining (6 per cent) in combination with high evaluating (22 per cent).

Potential strength
You assess needs realistically, and your judgment regarding priorities is sound. In a complex situation you have an instinctive talent for clarifying the issues. You are not motivated to apply pressure or sheer power of will to gain your ends.

Potential weakness
Realise that you are not highly motivated to stand your ground if opposed or openly attacked. You may be too flexible and accommodating towards other's views.

Possible action
1. Protect yourself by seeking support when faced with the possibility of opposition.
2. Be confident in your ability to clarify issues and see needs with crystal clarity.
3. Assess your reasons for being accommodating if you find yourself behaving in this way too often. Be determined to stand firm if necessary.

1.4 Timing highest (29 per cent) coupled with moderate anticipating (14 per cent).

Potential strength
Your sense of timing is well developed and you set the pace according to needs. You enjoy a fast pace and take quick advantage of new opportunities as they arise.

Potential weakness
In your eagerness to get things moving you may pre-empt others in decision-making. You are likely to feel impatient with those who need to take their time to

reach a decision. There is some danger that you may neglect long-term goals in favour of short-term results.

Possible action
1. Make sure you are fully aware of long-term company goals.
2. Consider whether taking advantage of some opportunities takes you too far from company goals.
3. Ensure that responsibility for decision-making is clearly defined within your own sphere of authority. Where others clearly have the responsibility for decision-making do not step in and take control unless it is imperative.

1.5 Your strengths are investigating (23 per cent), evaluating (22 per cent) and timing (29 per cent).

Potential strength
Your action is based on a sound appreciation of needs and a detailed, precise knowledge of the necessary facts. You bring an exceptional degree of clarity to interpretation of your responsibility, enabling you to take the appropriate action at the right time. You are likely to promote a highly competitive atmosphere.

Potential weakness
You may be too concerned with achieving results and fail to appreciate adequately those whose main achievements are in the realm of ideas or smooth administration.

Possible action
1. Reward and/or praise your staff for achieving results, thus emphasising the positive side of the competitive atmosphere you promote.
2. Broaden your ideas of achievement to include promoting creative ideas, smooth administration, awareness of trends, forward planning and other abstract forms of talent.

1.6 Low exploring (6 per cent) together with low determining (6 per cent) and moderate anticipating (14 per cent).

Potential strength
In planning action your approach is to maintain clarity of vision and freedom from distraction. Your flexibility enables you to change course in order to take advantage of changing situations.

Potential weakness
Realise that you may not be fully aware of approaching difficulties, nor find it easy to think of alternative ways to overcome them. You also have little motivation to stand your ground. This combination of traits means that you could be somewhat nonplussed if faced with unexpected trouble.

Possible Action
1. Apart from seeking support from others when faced with 'difficulties (*see* 1.3) make use of creative members of your staff (who are high in exploring) to give you alternative ideas and ways out of such situations (*see* 1.2).
2. Take time to consider consequences before taking action.

1.7 Moderate identifying.

Potential strength
You are able to maintain a degree of detachment in dealing, for example, with a crisis.

Potential weakness
Others may find you a bit difficult to engage.

Possible action
Be open about your need to stand back and take a slightly detached view of events and people. See it as an aid to maintaining a position of authority.

Investigating	$\leq 7.$	
ATTENTION Exploring	$10 7.$	
Determining	$30 7.$	
INTENTION		
Evaluating	$25 7.$	
Timing	$15 7.$	
COMMITMENT		
Anticipating	$15 7.$	

Action Profile of Mr T. Bayer. Adaptability low, identifying strong.

MR T. BAYER

Mr T. Bayer was the vice president/sales of a small American manufacturer of consumer products. He had been with the company all his career, starting as a sales representative and gaining steady promotion.

At the time this Profile was drawn the American company had just been purchased by an English manufacturing concern. The new owners were considering whether to promote Mr Bayer to chief executive officer or recruit a CEO from outside the firm. The Profile was done to help assess Mr Bayer's potential for the role for which he was being considered.

ACTION PROFILE REPORT

1.1   Intention highest (55 per cent) with commitment moderate (30 per cent) and attention low (15 per cent).

Potential strength
You know your own mind with great self-conviction and you can be extremely successful in persevering until you reach your objectives. You do not allow yourself to become bogged down in preliminary details.

Potential weakness
You tend to form opinions before all the facts are in. Your tenacious determination may make you inflexible, not permitting you to switch your energies according to developing possibilities.

Possible action

1. Take time to check information and consider alternatives before making up your mind on an issue.

2. Rely on others to contribute information and ideas during preliminary consideration of a project.

1.2 Low investigating (5 per cent) and low exploring (10 per cent).

Potential strength
You are not inclined to analyse things too closely or to nit-pick over unimportant details. You will stick to the tried and true rather than experimenting with the new and innovative.

Potential weakness
You run the risk of drawing erroneous conclusions because you simply don't take the time to get accurate information. You may behave inflexibly out of an unwillingness to look for or consider alternative ideas.

Possible action

1. Depend on others to establish methods, define standards and check for precision.

2. Have others feed you the information you need to make a decision.

3. Work to develop a more penetrating observatory power.

4. Before you make up your mind ask yourself, "Is there another way to do this?"

1.3 Timing and anticipating moderate (15 per cent each).

Potential strength
You are forward-looking in envisioning an objective. You are able to pursue your objectives without creating a competitive environment.

Potential weakness
You are liable to come to an agreement which leaves you uncommitted on aspects of timing.

Possible action
   1. Be sure that in persevering with your objectives you do not slacken pace or schedule intermediate steps haphazardly.
   2. Rely on others more adept than you at timing and anticipating to cue you as to when to act and to help you update plans.

1.4   High determining (30 per cent) with high evaluating (25 per cent).

Potential strength
You will be persistent, and highly motivated to stand your ground if faced with opposition. You have an innate sense for what is important You are not afraid to face up to hard facts and to deal with priorities in a realistic way.

Potential weakness
You may not be flexible enough in accommodating other views and opinions.

Possible action
   1. Recognise that you are well-equipped to handle situations that call for tenacious persistence and self-discipline.
   2. Recognise that you are highly persuasive and may be seen as overwhelming by colleagues whose convictions are weaker than yours. Cultivate your approachability and be wary of bullying others to agree with your point of view.

1.5   Low investigating (5 per cent), and exploring (10 per cent) together with moderate timing and anticipating (15 per cent each).

Potential strength
In planning action, your approach is to avoid becoming entangled or distracted by too many details or ideas. This gives you the freedom to take advantage of opportunities and changing situations.

Potential weakness
Realise that you run the risk of being dangerously uninformed and that this can cause you to make slipshod decisions.

Possible action
Rely on others to keep you informed and alert to possibilities arising from your actions.

1.6   Adaptability low.

Potential strength
You will not be over accommodating or malleable in a new and unfamiliar setting, particularly if accommodation means altering matters of policy or deeply felt beliefs.

Potential weakness
You will tend to demand that the world think as you think. In a rapidly changing situation you may wind up in an untenable position.

Possible action
   1. Where possible stick with a tried and true situation in which you know the ropes and have been successful.
   2. In a new or different situation make an extra effort to stay abreast of change and to be well-informed before acting.

NOTE: Following the Action Profile report from the consultant the owners decided to recruit a more committed CEO from outside. Mr Bayer has remained with the company in a sales and marketing capacity and is regarded as being quite successful.

CONCLUSION

These two case histories, chosen because of the contrasting styles of the two men, give some indication of the specificity with which Action Profiles can describe decision-making style. The reports also suggest some of the ways individuals can use the information to enhance their strengths and bolster themselves where they are weak.

The specificity and utility of the Action Profile are the result of 30 years of research and development carried on by Warren Lamb and his associates. How the Action Profile reached its current level of sophistication is a fascinating story which will be described in the next chapter.

CHAPTER 4

The Development of the Action Profile

THE BIRTH OF AN IDEA

We are now going to take a jump backwards and downwards — back in time and down from the executive offices to the factory line — to investigate the origins of Action Profiling.

Around the turn of this century the acceleration in the standardisation of parts and mass production forced scientists to begin looking at a hitherto unstudied aspect of industrialisation, the movements of the line worker. Of course the goal of these studies was to enhance the efficiency of the workers' movements, to lower production costs and to raise profits, and the initial thrust of this time and motion research dealt with quantitative problems. The aim was to move goods the shortest distance possible and to cut out unnecessary motions made by the operatives. The study was conducted by filming line workers in action, analysing what they were doing and then working reductively to cut out any unnecessary movements.

We now move to wartime England in the early 1940s. Problem number one: with a lot of the male workforce fighting in the war, women had to be trained to do factory line work previously done by men. Problem number two: because of the war there was a film shortage which was inhibiting the time and motion experts.

Enter Rudolf Laban, Hungarian teacher and movement researcher recently fled from Nazi Germany. Earlier in the century, in 1928, Laban had invented a notation system which could be used to record human movements. Word of Laban's arrival in Manchester reached F.C. Lawrence, a management consultant. Lawrence latched on to Laban and his ideas, and began to take him into his clients' factories to study and notate workers' movements.

Laban's original movement analysis work had concentrated on the structural aspects of motion: which part of the body is in motion, where it moves in the space around the body and how long it takes to reach its destination. Once in the factories, however, Laban became more interested in energy usage. He reasoned that it was the dynamic aspects of movement, the energetic rhythm of exertion and recuperation, which had the most effect on a worker's efficiency. By finding new rhythms for doing the work Laban was able to train women to take on some heavy jobs previously done by men.

After the war Laban continued to test his ideas on efficiency with the help of his student, Warren Lamb. They went to work in the factories of the Lancashire textile industry where they would make notations of a worker's effort rhythms and then compare these notations with his or her production record. The simple goal was to determine the correct effort rhythm for a particular line job, find a worker with a particular aptitude who could be trained in that rhythm and then to match the two up.

Lamb writes of this time:

"The usual practice was for me to work alone, standing all day in some hot steamy shed, the clatter of looms making speech impossible, intensely observing

... . Laban demanded lots of sheets of paper covered with effort 'graphs' (notations) and I strove desperately to make copious observations of some sort or other. The usual practice was for me to take these sheets of paper to Laban, who would go through them avidly asking me penetrating questions. He would try out various ways of analysing the observations. Preliminary conclusions would be reached ... mainly as to who was suitable and who wasn't. Then Laban would accompany me to the scene and would confirm or refute the conclusions after a quick look at the subjects."

This work with operatives led to the odd foreman or manager being included. Lamb writes:

"Laban had a guru-like charisma and so managers who felt themselves in some difficulty would consult him. Laban used his genius for giving some point of advice which, when the manager tried it out, helped him to feel better. When inconvenient to Laban, I would find myself observing a manager's movement and sometimes making a report."

The principle being applied to the manager was the same as that used with an operative. The rhythms of an individual's movement on the job were notated and analysed, then the movement profile was compared to a job description and finally some prediction was attempted as to the manager's suitability for the job. Gradually it was discovered that during a meeting or an interview with a manager a rhythmic pattern could be observed which was identical to his or her on-the-job pattern. Watching the manager doing actual work was therefore dropped and instead observations were taken during a standard interview.

*It has been discovered that observations made in the course of a
standard interview reveal the same rhythmic patterns of movement
exhibited on the job.*

DEVELOPING THE IDEA

In 1952 Lamb opened his own management consultancy
practice and from this time onwards he developed his
movement profiling techniques independently of
Laban. This development occurred along two lines.

Firstly, Lamb compiled extremely detailed job
descriptions reflecting the attention–intention–commitment model of decision-making which had been put
forward by Laban. Thus Lamb considered three
questions:

1. To what did the manager have to give attention on
   the job?
2. What did he have to resolve?
3. What action did he have to initiate?

From these questions Lamb would compile a job
description consisting of thirty or forty different items.

Secondly, this complicated job description was then compared with the movement profile, which Lamb was also developing. Laban had only identified the movement elements which related to assertion in decision-making. Lamb was able to identify the movement elements which related to perspective by combining careful observation, theorising and his growing experience in the field.

Over a fifteen-year period, making several thousand movement assessments, Lamb gradually refined both the observation technique and the interpretative framework. A profile, believed by Lamb to reveal managerial aptitude, was formulated and called an Aptitude Assessment. This name was later changed to Action Profile at the suggestion of Pamela Ramsden, but that's the next step in the story.

VALIDATING THE IDEA

By 1970 Lamb had assessed nearly 4,000 managers. One long-standing client company that had been using Lamb's Aptitude Assessments for 15 years wanted further research done on the technique, and to this end research psychologist Pamela Ramsden was hired to conduct a validation study.

What Ramsden clarified in her research was that the behaviour being tapped was *motivational* rather than *aptitudinal*. Her studies revealed that the Action Profile represents the individual's drive to take initiative during certain stages of decision-making. The Profile could predict what an individual needed to "put in" to a decision. This meant that the Profile showed a manager's *pattern of preferred initiatives* as it related to internal motivation.

Ramsden clarified this point by correlating Lamb's work with Abraham Maslow's work on motivation.

Maslow, an American behavioural scientist, theorised that human needs are hierarchical in nature: physiological needs are the most basic, followed by psychological and social needs, and finally crowned by the need for self-actualisation. The ascending order of this hierarchy is shown below.

Need for self-actualisation (highest need).
Need for esteem.
Need for belonging and love.
Safety needs.
Physiological needs (most basic need).

Maslow believed that an individual's behaviour is organised around his *unsatisfied* needs. This means that once a need is satisfied it no longer motivates the individual. For example, it is often said that "Man does not live by bread alone", but according to Maslow this is only true of the man who *has* bread. The man whose stomach is cavernously empty is likely to be completely dominated by thoughts of bread and the need to find food will be his strongest motivation. However, once the man's stomach is full Maslow suggests that the motivation to find food will vanish and will be replaced by a higher need, such as locating a safe place to live, finding a loving companion, winning a bowling trophy or even a Nobel Prize. And so it goes on. As physiological requirements, safety, belonging, love and esteem are supplied, their power as motivational forces evaporates.

The one exception to this vanishing motivation phenomena is the need to self-actualise. Self-actualisation can be thought of as the need to fulfil one's potential. Just as fish must swim and birds must fly, so what a man *can* be he *must* be. This need "to be what he must be" is a drive which is not dispelled by achievement. According to Maslow self-actualisation is continuously motivational.

When considering work, self-actualisation can be seen as the drive to find a job that is not just lucrative or prestigious but is interesting as well. Idealistically speaking, self-actualising work is the kind of work one would do even without pay simply because the work itself is fulfilling and enjoyable. Needless to say, one man's self-actualising job is another man's poison, job satisfaction being a very individual matter. And this is where the Action Profile comes in.

Job satisfaction is a highly individual matter.

Ramsden reasoned that the Profile did not reveal managerial aptitude per se, as aptitude is often a combination of natural talent and acquired skill. Moreover, one can have an aptitude and not be motivated to apply it. What Ramsden discovered in her research was that the Action Profile indicated *where an individual will be motivated to apply his aptitudes*. For example, an attention-oriented manager will be motivated to ferret out information and look for alternatives. A job which emphasises this preliminary stage of decision-making will give him the greatest scope for self-actualisation. On the other hand, the

Action Profiles reveal motivational rather than aptitudinal behaviours. They show a pattern of preferred initiatives.

commitment-oriented executive will want to be in the thick of the fray, executing action rather than considering it, and a job involving decisive implementation provides him with the scope for self-actualisation.

Because the Profile shows what an individual's input in a decision-making process will be, it makes it possible to place an executive in a role where he or she is able to take the kind of initiatives that are most fulfilling. Moreover, if the individual continues to act in accordance with the pattern of preferred initiatives indicated by the Profile, the job will continue to be fulfilling as the pattern represents self-actualising needs which are always motivational.

SUMMARY

During World War II, Rudolf Laban hypothesised that efficiency in line work was related to an operative's ability to perform certain dynamic "effort" rhythms. This ability could be perceived through observation of the operative at work.

Laban's student and colleague, Warren Lamb, began to apply this practice to his consultancy work with senior managers. By interviewing 4,000 managers and studying their body movements Lamb developed the Action Profile, which he believed revealed certain types of managerial aptitude. By correlating these aptitudes with the demands of the job, Lamb believed he could predict an individual's effectiveness.

Pamela Ramsden was hired to validate the Action Profile and her research provided a clear theoretical framework for the work that had been started almost 20 years earlier. By correlating Maslow's theories with Lamb's observations and experience in the field, Ramsden was able to formulate the theory of Action Motivation. This theory proposed that the Action Profile represented an individual manager's self-actualising need to be involved at certain stages of the decision-making process. This meant that the Profile indicated *how* a person preferred to make decisions. It indicated management style.

Ramsden's work confirmed the use of the Action Profile as a means for understanding management behaviour. Aptitude, how well an executive can do his job, is related to his intelligence, his education and his experience. These factors can be easily assessed by I.Q. testing, interviewing, studying the man's records, and so on. Self-actualising motivation and decision-making style, however, cannot be assessed by these methods. An individual's action motivation can best be understood by carefully studying his actions. In other words it is movement which reveals decision-making style.

In the following chapter we will describe how movement is perceived, recorded and interpreted in order to analyse a manager's action motivation and to make his Action Profile.

PART TWO
Movement and Motivation

CHAPTER 5

Movement and Internal Motivation

MOVEMENT AS COMMUNICATION

"Movement thinking could be considered as a gathering of impressions of happenings in one's own mind, for which nomenclature is lacking."

Rudolf Laban

Body language is a term coined in recent years to refer to body movement and its meanings. The term has popularised the concept that movement is a language, that it is one of humankind's major means of communication. By implication the term "body language" suggests that movement is analogous to verbal language in its significance and structure, but in reality this is simply not true. What movement denotes, its connotations and how it's structure gives rise to meaningful sequences differs fundamentally from the structures and meaning of words. Understanding these differences between verbal and non-verbal communication is the key to understanding how Action Profiles are made and interpreted.

ABSTRACT SYMBOLS

Words are abstract representations of things, ideas and actions. Very few words sound like what they mean, and even fewer words look like what they mean. Sheer perception — hearing and seeing words — is not enough to understand their meaning, as any visitor to a foreign country can attest. Understanding verbal language involves cognition because words are abstract symbols for experience.

Movement, on the other hand, does represent things, ideas and actions directly. The perceptual elements of motion, its force, direction, duration, rhythm, the appearance and bodily sensation of the action, make up its meaning. Movement *is* what it seems. Movement *does* what is says. Movement is not abstract.

NAMING THINGS

Words make it possible to break experiences down into comprehensible parts which have names and commonly understood definitions. Those named parts can then be arranged in some kind of order and used to communicate personal experience to others.

Movement, on the other hand, carries the kind of information that cannot be conveyed by words. This is why it is often impossible to explain a dance, to capture the nuance of a gesture or to describe a certain body carriage in words. Movement expresses those parts of experience for which there are no names. As Laban said, movement deals with those "happenings in one's own mind for which nomenclature is lacking". Moreover, movement communicates those nameless happenings in its own unique structural form.

STRUCTURE

Written and spoken language is arranged linearly. A sentence deals with one event at a time, often portraying a cause and effect relationship, e.g. John (subject) grasped (verb) the suitcase (object). Complex sentences make it possible to draw logical relationships between these cause and effect sequences, e.g. While she was stirring the batter the doorbell rang and the dog began to bark, waking the baby. But even in a complex sentence there is still a linear structure. It is not possible, verbally, to place two or more events in a sequence simultaneously. Consider this sentence: The man peered forward into the gloom, hunching his shoulders. Although the man "peered" and "hunched" at the same moment, one action follows the other in the sentence structure. Only poetry, which violates syntax, can imply simultaneity.

Verbal language forces the speaker or writer to break experience down into named parts and then to structure the parts sequentially. This makes it possible to communicate the experience in an orderly fashion, detail by detail.

Movement, on the other hand, does not communicate experience in an orderly fashion, detail by detail, because movement occurs in "irrational" clusters. This clustering has been termed *felt sense* by psychiatrist Eugene Gendlin. In a passage which has much in common with Laban's concept of "movement thinking" Gendlin describes felt sense in the following way.

"A felt sense is not a mental experience but a physical one. Physical. A bodily awareness of a situation or person or event. An initial aura that encompasses everything you feel and know about the given subject at a given time — encompasses it and communicates it to you all at once rather than detail by detail."

Every movement involves some change in the body's energy, some change in direction, and some variation in its coordination. These complex clusters of change carry many levels of meaning. When an individual suddenly crosses his arms and curls backwards into an easy chair, various meanings are suggested simultaneously. The movement may mean, "I'm restless and need to shift my position," or "I'm protecting myself by retreating", or "I've reached a decision," or something else. Even this simple everyday action creates a complex impression that is rich in its simultaneous effects.

What we are suggesting is that movement deals with those experiences which are verbally inexpressible. We are saying that body language has its own unique structure. We are asserting that movement has a different expressive function to that of words. And we believe that, among other things, movement reveals decision-making style. The large composites of behaviour which we call action motivation or management style are composed of thousands of movement clusters. These movement clusters make up an action pattern which is characteristic of the individual's decision-making manner.

In the following chapters we will examine these movement clusters, analyse the changes in the body's rhythm and direction and see what movement can tell us about individual motivation.

CHAPTER 6

The Articulate Body

The body in motion is like a visual symphony. The head, trunk, limbs and extremities, like sections of an orchestra, weave and interweave their melodies in varying patterns. Sometimes a single body part will take a solo, as in swinging the lower leg or tilting the head. Sometimes body parts move contrapuntally; the head nods slowly while the fingers tap a rapid tattoo. The body can sculpt itself into a shape and pause, statuelike, or all body parts may be brought into play simultaneously, as in a well coordinated leap or a sudden, startled shrinking.

These examples point to three major ways in which the body can orchestrate itself: in gestures, in postures, or in phrases in which postures and gestures are merged.

GESTURES

A gesture is a solo for a single body part. When the arm moves without disturbing the position of the rest of the body we call it a gesture. When the lips spread into a smile without a muscle rippling in the shoulders or chest we call it a gesture. When the whole torso tilts to the side without a flicker of motion in the legs we call it a gesture. A gesture is a motion confined to one or two parts of the body.

A gesture is a solo for a single body part.

Obviously, millions of human activities fit into this category. Any activity, from tap dancing to diamond cutting to proposing marriage, can be performed as a series of gestures. This ability to isolate an action to one part of the body with precise differentiation and articulation makes possible a great range of functional tasks and expressive actions.

Gestures are not always confined to single parts of the body, however; often two or more gestures may occur simultaneously. This frequently happens in conversation. One may shrug one's shoulders while uncrossing one's legs without involving the head, arms, or torso, or one can nod the head and wiggle the foot without a tremor of motion rippling the rest of the body.

Gestures can be learned. The one-man band, pounding a drum, grazing a cymbal, puffing a harmonica and tinkling a triangle, has, through practice, developed his simultaneous gesturing to the level of a virtuoso. The gestures of a political candidate are carefully groomed. Adolescents imitate their favourite film and rock stars, while practically all of us have caught ourselves, at one time or another, copying the mannerism of a friend or colleague.

Gestures are eminently imitable. They can be learned and unlearned. Much like a suit of clothes, one can put on a gesture or take it off at whim. Gestures have display power. They can be used to affect a genuineness which is not actually felt. This is what is implied by the idiomatic expression "making the gesture".

For the reasons enumerated above, the meaning of a brisk nod, an energetically twitching foot or a vivid smile can only be deduced from the context in which the gesture occurs. And even then, one must be something of a mind reader to judge accurately whether the gesture is a momentary disguise or a genuine expression.

No fixed meanings are assigned to specific gestures and therefore the Action Profiler must be careful to differentiate between gestures and other wider uses of the body.

POSTURES

A posture is a pose or position assumed by the whole body. Two types of postures can be distinguished: those which are momentarily held arrangements of body parts; and those which are chronically "fixed" body shapes.

Normal conversation is punctuated by postures of the first variety. A stiffly erect posture dissolves into a more relaxed sprawled position. This ends up as a condensed

A posture is a pose or position assumed by the whole body.

and twisted pose, to be followed by a return to the erect stance, and so on. Like commas and full stops, these postures are momentary pauses in the flow of action.

These brief rests often facilitate verbal exchange. They help to signal changes of subject in the conversation and act to indicate whose turn it is to speak. Read in the context of verbal exchange, these momentarily-held positions may also indicate the emotional responses of those taking part in the conversation. Once again, because these postures are context-dependent, no attempt is made to fix specific meanings to them when constructing an Action Profile.

The second type of posture, the chronically fixed body shape, conforms more to the old-fashioned idea of body carriage. These chronic postures can be typified by the alignment of the head, chest, waist and pelvis along the vertical axis of the body. Unlike momentary postures, these alignments cannot be altered at will but are constantly present. These poses can be thought of as the key signature that underlies the orchestration of all other body parts. For example, one man may maintain an aggressive forward thrust of his chin even when he is in a calmly receptive mood. Another individual may hold his chest in a sunken, concave position even when being honoured with a Nobel prize. A model may pose off-camera as well as on with her pelvis thrust forward and her shoulders held back.

Because of the chronic nature of these postures they are often referred to as "body attitudes". Body attitude is a kind of postural base-line from which other postures and gestures develop. Body attitude may be indicative of psychological factors such as self-image (a hangdog stance), of postural adjustments to work (the stoop of someone who sweeps floors or roads) or of cultural traits (the ram-rod straight Victorian). However, body attitude is not indicative of decision-making style and is therefore, yet again, disregarded in the making and interpretation of Action Profiles.

POSTURE/GESTURE MERGERS
OR INTEGRATED MOVEMENTS

A posture/gesture merger is an action which involves movement throughout the body. The motion either begins as a gesture and spreads through the body or it begins posturally with a whole body action and diminishes to an isolated gesture.

Posture/gesture mergers are often called integrated movements because the quality or shape of the body action is consistent. As if cut from the same piece of cloth, the variations in time, force, focus and direction of the gesture are the same as those of the posture.

Posture/gesture mergers are similar to postures in that they involve the whole body, but they are not still or frozen; these integrated movements are constantly moving and changing. They also differ from gestures in their involvement of the whole body, all body parts being utilised. This activation may be slight, but there will be a hint of stirring throughout the body or a tremor of energy in all the limbs.

In simultaneous gestures the whole body may indeed be in motion, but the rhythm and shape of each gesture will not be consistent with one another. It is the cohesion of rhythm and shape in the whole body that characterises posture/gesture mergers.

Posture/gesture mergers often highlight longer movement sequences. A gesture may begin such a sequence, subsequently merging into an integrated action as the dynamic quality spreads through the whole body. Imagine touching a hot stove: a startled raising of the hand is followed by an alarmed retreat as the whole body recoils suddenly. The dynamic quality of this quick gestural response is echoed in an accelerated action of the whole body. Or picture a sequence in which someone projects his whole torso forward in the chair and then gestures in front of himself with his left arm. In this example the sequence of actions develops from the posture to the gesture and it is the sculptural aspect which becomes integrated.

We mentioned before that movement is directly

expressive, that body actions look and feel like what they mean. This meaning of integrated movement arises from the consistent involvement of the whole body. At a symbolic level, moments of integrated movement imply that the whole person is involved in the activity. This is borne out empirically in that a person will perform integrated movements with greater frequency when discussing a topic which is of particular interest to him than when engaging in polite but disinterested chitchat.

Posture/gesture mergers are innate, natural and individualistic. These movements make up the larger behavioural patterns which characterise an individual's decision-making style.

Posture/gesture mergers can occur in practically any activity, but whether they do or do not and what they are like is a highly individual matter. An individual's posture/gesture mergers can be seen to occur and re-occur in repeating, even predictable, patterns, yet the individual is often quite unaware of and unselfconscious about these integrated movements.

Moreover, while gestures can be learned and postures assumed, it is very difficult to imitate accurately another person's integrated movements. Attempts have been made to train individuals to perform posture/gesture mergers, but these attempts have met with only limited success. There seems to be something innate, natural and highly individualistic about integrated movement.

It is for these reasons that Action Profile interpretation is based upon observation of posture/ gesture mergers. The unique, inimitable pattern and composition of these groups of integrated movements make up the large behavioural patterns which characterise an individual's decision-making style.

In the following chapters we will delineate the qualities which colour integrated movements and explain how these qualities relate to management style.

CHAPTER 7

The Dynamics of Action

Distance, force and time are mechanical factors which affect all physical movement, including the body movements of human beings. Human movements can be analysed from a mechanical point of view, where the body is seen as an engine moving a set of weights and bony levers, overcoming inertia and gravity and resisting momentum. From this viewpoint human movement appears to be a marvellous *ballet mechanique*, and also a quantitatively measurable phenomenon.

However, in Action Profiling we are dealing with movement as a communication system, not a mechanical phenomenon. Consequently, what interests us is not what is mechanically measurable but rather what is perceived by the naked but informed eye. It is the quality of movement, not the quantity, which captures the attention of the Action Profiler.

Although the human engine is governed by factors of distance, force and time, the human being has the power to vary these factors qualitatively. These qualitative variations swing between two poles. Quantitative and qualitative factors of motion are shown in the table below. Please note that a fourth qualitative factor, called flow, was defined by Laban. This factor is related to quantitatively measurable levels of muscle tension, and is included in the table.

Quantitative factors	Qualitative factors
Distance	Varying focus[1]
	Directing ⟷ Indirecting
Force	Varying pressure[2]
	Increasing pressure ⟷ Decreasing pressure
Time	Varying pace[3]
	Accelerating ⟷ Decelerating
Tension	Varying flow
	Binding ⟷ Freeing

Each of these qualitative factors can be related to one of the basic management styles we have discussed in Chapter 2. These correlations have been discovered through direct observation of the behaviour of senior managers.

VARYING FOCUS

Varying focus provides a means of orientating oneself physically, of zeroing in on something of interest either in a straightforward direct way or in a flexible indirect way. For example, when an individual enters a room he has never been in before he will usually orientate himself with focusing movements. He may scan the room first, taking it all in and getting a general impression. This kind of indirect focusing activity usually *seems* to involve only vision, but it would be wrong to think of it as a purely visual happening; the whole body can participate by sensing the proportions of the room, the possibilities for motion, where large objects are located, etc.

One can also orientate oneself by homing in on objects of particular interest and channelling movement in a definite direction. Instead of many foci of equal

1. Focus was originally called the space effort by Laban.
2. Pressure was originally called the weight effort by Laban.
3. Pace was originally called the time effort by Laban.

interest there is only one focus, and movement becomes straight and direct.

A directing movement indicates an orientation to the environment that is channelled, precise and pinpointed. Such a movement occurs without any deviation in course. A directing movement is often spoken of as having a single spatial focus; it is straight, aimed, unswerving. An indirecting movement, on the other hand, is circuitous, roundabout, looping. Such a movement follows a more sinuous, serpentine pathway. Indirecting movements have the effect of scanning the environment, taking in many focal points at once.

The ability to change the orientation of oneself in relation to a space, an object or a person, through variations in focus, makes many functional and expressive actions possible.

1. Functional activities in which directing movements may be used are threading a needle, painting the edge of a door frame, striking a nail on the head or aiming and throwing darts.

2. Expressive examples of directing movements include the following: precisely positioning an object on a desk; drawing lines in the air while describing an object; walking through a crowded street as if wearing blinkers; and pointing out directions to a lost motorist.

3. Indirecting movements might occur in the following functional actions: spooning whipped cream out of a bowl; slashing weeds in a garden; tying a shoe lace; or feeling around for a light switch in the dark.

4. Peering around to find a familiar face at a crowded cocktail party, tilting and turning one's head while considering a question, thoughtfully twirling a strand of hair or wringing one's hands are all examples of expressive actions in which indirecting movements might play a role.

Variations in focus reveal an investigative action motivation.

THE MEANING OF FOCUS VARIATIONS

The readiness to vary focus in integrated whole-body actions reveals an investigative management style. As we have mentioned before, the investigative manager is characteristically curious, inquisitive and analytical, and this felt sense is expressed physically by variations in focus. The investigative manager directs, probing for information; he indirects, scanning and categorising data. This physical tendency to orientate oneself by changing focus reveals a need to act in an investigative manner.

VARYING PRESSURE

Qualitative variations in pressure add enormously to the range of what a person can do with his or her actual weight and muscular strength. In pressure variations the individual actually appears to add to or subtract from the mass, weight and strength nature has given to him. This explains why the 90-pound weakling can have a forceful stride or the 200-pounder appear to move as gracefully as a feather.

In movements of increasing pressure one capitalises on the forces of compression which work on the body, using weight and muscle power to produce forceful exertion. Actions of increasing pressure look strong, mighty, powerful, solid. Decreasing pressure capitalises on the tensile forces of suspension. One rarefies one's weight, seeming to defy gravity. Actions of decreasing pressure appear to be light, delicate, airy, buoyant. Pressure variations facilitate a vast number of functional and expressive tasks.

1. Functional actions which may require increasing pressure are rubbing the spots off a dirty table-top, unscrewing a tight jar-lid, pounding on an ancient manual typewriter and cutting a thick piece of cardboard.

2. Squeezing a loved one's hand, slamming down the phone receiver in indignation, whipping off a jacket and hurling it into a nearby chair and pressing one's palms together thoughtfully are all expressive actions in which increasing pressure plays a role.

3. Examples of functional actions which might require decreasing pressure are tiptoeing into a room where someone is sleeping, smoothing a piece of tissue paper, tracing fine lines on onion-skin paper and icing a cake with whipped cream.

4. Kissing the tip of someone's nose, delicately tapping one's fingers on a table-top, dabbing one's eyes with a handkerchief and gently guiding an elderly person to a chair are expressive movements involving decreasing pressure.

THE MEANING OF PRESSURE VARIATIONS

The readiness to vary pressure in integrated whole-body

Variations in pressure reveal a determined action motivation.

actions reveals a determined management style. The determined manager is characteristically resolute and purposeful, and this felt sense is expressed physically in variations in pressure. The conviction that a certain thing must be done can take hold of one either powerfully and firmly or gently and persistently. The physical tendency to exert pressure in varying degrees, to convince oneself or persuade others, reveals a need to act in a determined manner.

VARYING PACE

Pace is related to, but not synonomous with, tempo. Tempo can be fast or slow, but once set it is maintained evenly, i.e. the tempo of the action proceeds at a uniform speed which can be quantitatively measured. Pace, as defined here, deals with perceptible variations in speed. Pace is the process of changing tempo, of accelerating or decelerating the speed of a motion.

Accelerating a movement involves abruptly speeding it up. Such movement is sudden, unexpected, instantaneous, fleeting. It is as if time itself were condensed.

Accelerating movements have a staccato-like spark of urgency. Decelerating a movement, however, involves gradually slowing down its tempo as if to prolong the action. Such movement is lingering, leisurely, unhurried. It is as if time were drawn out. Decelerating movements have a languid, adagio quality.

The ability to vary pace makes many functional and expressive activities possible.

1. Functional actions which might utilise accelerating are testing a hot iron with a fingertip, catching a glass before it crashes to the floor, flicking away a mosquito and springing through an elevator door just before it closes.

2. Giving a startled jerk on hearing an unexpected noise, excitedly tearing open an envelope, suddenly clicking one's fingers in irritation at forgetting something and curtly ending a phone conversation with a quick "Gotta go" are all examples of expressive actions where accelerating plays a role.

3. Functional activities which might involve decelerating include wringing out a heavy towel, gliding to a stop on ice skates, removing a bandage gradually and cautiously shaving with a new razor blade.

4. Soothing a frightened animal, sinking into an easy chair after a hard day, desultorily shrugging one's shoulders and yawning lazily are examples of expressive actions in which decelerating plays a role.

THE MEANING OF PACE VARIATIONS

The ability to vary pace in integrated whole-body actions reveals a time-keeping management style. The time-keeping manager is a go-getter — prompt, methodical, competitive — and this felt sense is expressed physically by variations in pace. The time-keeper controls the pacing of implementation; he speeds up and slows down

Variations in pace reveal a time-keeping action motivation.

action in order to move at the most appropriate
moment. This physical tendency to alter the pacing of
commitment reveals a need to act in a time-keeping
manner.

TENSION FLOW VARIATIONS

All movement produces muscular tension; a muscle
works by contracting (tensing) and exerting a pull on the
bony lever to which it is attached. The term "flow" was

coined by Laban to describe the variations in the relationships between tensed muscles. Varying these relationships — binding or freeing flow — produces a perceptible difference in the look of a movement.

Bound flow occurs when both agonistic and antagonistic muscle groups contract and shorten. This opposed tension makes it possible to control a movement precisely. Binding the flow gives movement a controlled and restrained look, e.g. carrying cups brimful of boiling coffee, manoeuvring through a narrow aisle in a crowded china shop, removing a speck from someone's eye or miming the action of pushing a heavy box. Such movements can be stopped at any moment; their momentum is under control.

Free flow occurs when the agonistic muscle group contracts and the antagonistic group lengthens. This complementary tension produces freer, less controllable motion. Freeing the flow gives movement a fluent easy look, e.g. shaking out a duster, kicking a football, swinging a heavy object and whirling in an abandoned manner. These actions are hard to stop; they have an inherent momentum.

The greatest variation in flow is seen in the integrated whole-body actions of children. The wiggling, grasping, stretching and curling movements of an infant, the skipping, running and whirling movements of children at play, all feature freeing and binding of flow.

Child development studies have shown that the mastery of rhythmic variations in the freeing and binding of flow are crucial to the development of other motor skills. The infant who gleefully grasps a handful of food and hurls it on to the floor has just mastered a flow variation (bound to free), although his mother can scarcely be expected to share his glee as whole-heartedly. These integrated flow variations are thought to be the precursors of other dynamic qualities.

As children mature, focus, pressure and pace variations take precedence in integrated movements, while flow variations become less predominant. While this is a general trend, many adults do display a high incidence of integrated flow variation. This flow variation carries with it certain "childlike" qualities of spontaneity, enthusiasm and readiness to participate. For this reason, the amount of flow variation retained by an adult indicates his "response quotient" or level of sensitivity to the stimulation provided by the environment. Integrated flow variations indicate the individual's need to associate with the centres of activity in the company; that is, his level of identifying motivation.

SHAPE FLOW VARIATIONS

Besides free flow and bound changes in muscular tension, there is a second kind of flow related to changes in body shape. These changes are called shape flow.

First noted by Warren Lamb, shape flow varies from shrinking to growing. The basis of shape flow is seen in simple breathing. On exhalation the body shape appears to shrink a bit; on inhalation to grow slightly. Shape flow variations are body-oriented. In shrinking, the body shape contracts and shortens, becoming smaller, while the limbs fold inwards towards the body centre. In growing, the body shape expands and stretches, becoming larger, while the limbs appear to unfold, moving away from the body centre. All these variations can be quite subtle.

Stretching the spine and letting it compress again, wiggling while settling into a chair, bouncing impatiently while waiting for a lift and accommodating one's own body shape to another person's while embracing are all examples of variations in shape flow.

Like free flow and bound flow changes, growing and

shrinking predominate in the movement of children. In general, as children mature and learn to coordinate and articulate body movement better, shape flow diminishes. However, some adults do retain integrated shape flow variation to a high degree. This too, like tension flow, indicates the level of an individual's need to identify his own person with centres of activity at work.

SUMMARY

Quantitative factors of distance, force, time and tension correspond to certain qualitative factors which are relevant to Action Profiling. These kinetic qualities reveal particular kinds of action motivation. Correlations between movement and motivation are shown in the table below.

Dynamic quality	*Action motivation*
Varying focus reveals (directing ⟵⟶ indirecting)	Investigatory style
Varying pressure reveals (increasing ⟵⟶ decreasing pressure)	Determined style
Varying pace reveals (accelerating ⟵⟶ decelerating)	Time-keeping style
Varying flow reveals (binding ⟵⟶ freeing) (shrinking ⟵⟶ growing)	Intensity of need to identify self with activities in work environment.

As this table shows, focus, pressure and pace variations correspond to the more assertive decision-making styles. How then are the perspective-oriented styles indicated? The next chapter will reveal the answer to this question.

CHAPTER 8

Sculpting the Air

All movement produces sculptural changes in the body. Like all sculpture, the poetry of form lies in the interaction between the mass of the moving body and the empty space around it. The shapes the torso assumes are poignant. Its changing lines and swelling curves, its hollows and gently shifting convexities are particularly evocative. And difficult to capture, for unlike a bronze casting or a marble carving, the sculpture of movement is never still. The shapes are evanescent, evaporating even as they are formed.

To describe the sculpture of movement one needs to be able to map these disappearing shapes. This mapping process can be facilitated by visualising the space around the mover's body as a huge sphere. The limits of this spatial bubble, which we shall call the kinesphere, are the limits of reachable space available to a stationary mover, i.e. all the space one can reach without taking a step.

We can now create a three-dimensional "longitude and latitude" for the kinesphere which will help us to locate the spatial pathways of the body parts in motion. Let us imagine that the kinesphere is trisected by three planes. These planes intersect at the centre of the body and take their spatial orientation from the body (up is headwards, forward is nosewards, etc.). Each of these planes divides the kinesphere in half.

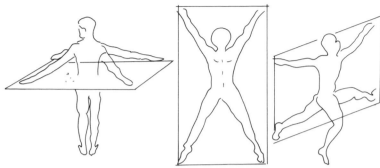

The table plane.   *The door plane.*   *The wheel plane.*

1. The table plane bisects the body at the waist level. Its primary dimension is width, its secondary dimension depth. It extends to the right and left and in front of and behind the body. It separates the head, chest and arms from the hips and legs.

2. The door plane slices vertically through the body from head to toe, separating the front of the body from the back. The door plane's primary dimension is height, its secondary dimension width. It extends up and down and to the right and left of the body.

3. The wheel plane bisects the body along its vertical axis, separating the right side from the left side. Its primary dimension is depth, its secondary dimension height. It extends in front of and behind the body, and also upwards and downwards.

Using these planes as points of reference, we can now describe the changing lines, curves and volumes described by the moving body.

While the mapping of these shapes is a fascinating and complex study, for Action Profiling we must distinguish posture/gesture mergers from those shape changes which are merely gestures.

In order to classify a posture/gesture merger the direction of the gesture must flow in the same direction as the shape change occurring in the whole body.

Moreover, one must see these sculptural variations as integrated within the shape of the torso. This means that the torso must actually change its concavities and convexities. An integrated shape change will produce new curving in the trunk.

These shape changes can be described by the plane in which they predominately lie.

SHAPING IN THE TABLE PLANE

Integrated movements lying in the table plane are described by the terms spreading and enclosing.

Spreading movements create a convex widening in the chest, waist and hips, as if one were sprawling back against a barrel. A spreading movement opens and reveals the body, creating an expanding perspective, as if one were scanning the horizon and staying in touch with what is happening on all sides.

The reversal of a spreading movement is an enclosing motion. Enclosing produces a concave shaping of the chest and waist, as if one were hugging a barrel. Enclosing movements have a quality of embracing space and of closing off the body. In an enclosing movement one surrounds the space in front of the body, establishing a perimeter or boundary.

Spreading and enclosing make many functional and expressive actions possible.

1. Spreading movements might be found in the following functional activities: scattering seeds in a field; hosing a garden; pushing aside high weeds while hiking; and reaching for the sleeve when someone is helping you on with a coat.

2. More expressive situations in which spreading might occur are the following: opening one's arms to embrace; sweeping someone out of the way; sprawling in a chair after a hard day; and swinging the arm

sideways and expanding the chest as if to demonstrate a vista of possibilities.

3. Functional actions in which an enclosing motion might occur include gathering up an armload of fresh laundry, winding oneself up to throw a ball, bringing someone down with a running tackle and polishing a desk-top with a circular motion.

4. Expressive uses of enclosing might include the following: scooping up a kitten and cradling it against one's chest; motioning someone to come nearer by making a sweeping horizontal arc with the arm; giving someone a bear hug; and crossing the leg and curving the body when saying "On the other hand ...".

Shaping in the table plane reveals an exploratory action motivation.

SHAPING IN THE TABLE PLANE — ITS MEANING

Integrated spreading and enclosing movements reveal an exploratory style. The exploratory manager is always on the lookout for something new; he just can't help searching out alternatives and trying to gain a new appreciation of the information available. This felt sense is expressed physically by shaping in the table plane, whereby spreading actions open the mover to new vistas and enclosing actions encompass new areas. The physical tendency to create horizontal, curving shapes in the table plane reveals a need to act in an exploratory manner.

SHAPING IN THE DOOR PLANE

Integrated movements in the door plane are described by the words rising and descending.

Rising movements involve an upwards and sideways curving of the body, as if the torso were leaning against a rainbow, one side of the torso becoming convex while the other side becomes concave. Because a rising movement emphasises an upwards direction, the curving is most pronounced through the ribs, chest and shoulder areas. Rising movements have an upward tilting and tipping quality.

The reversal of a rising motion is a descending shape. Descending movements produce a downwards and sideways curve in the torso, as if the body were fitting inside a crescent moon. Again, one side of the torso becomes concave while the other becomes convex, but, because descending emphasises a downwards motion, the curving is most pronounced through the waist and hips. Descending movements have a slanting, lowering, settling quality.

Rising and descending facilitate a variety of functional and expressive tasks.

1. Functional actions which involve rising might include the following: polishing a plate glass window; raising one's hand to attract a teacher's attention; tipping upwards to counterbalance a heavy suitcase; and reaching overhead while leaning sideways in a calisthenic exercise.

2. Expressive actions involving rising might include leaning sideways to rest one's head on someone's shoulder, raising one shoulder in a shrug, tilting one's head quizzically or drawing oneself up, arms akimbo, to confront an insulting person.

3. Descending could appear in the following functional actions: reaching sideways to catch a low ball; holding a door open with one's hip; lowering oneself to slide into a car; and leaning to the side to pick up a heavy suitcase.

4. Expressive actions involving descending might include snuggling up to someone seated on a couch, provocatively dropping the weight on to one hip when standing, poking someone in the ribs with an elbow and sinking sideways into a chair while crossing the arms as if to say "you can't get past me".

Shaping in the door plane reveals an evaluative action motivation.

SHAPING IN THE DOOR PLANE — ITS MEANING

Integrated movements in the door plane reveal an evaluative decision-making style. The critical and discerning evaluator aims to keep things in proportion.

He is always establishing clear priorities and arranging proposals in order of ascending and descending importance. This felt sense is expressed physically by shaping in the door plane. By rising, one towers above the issues; by descending, one shrinks beneath them, creating a different feeling of proportion. The physical tendency to create vertical, curving door plane shapes reveals a need to act in an evaluative manner.

SHAPING IN THE WHEEL PLANE

Integrated movements in the wheel plane are described by the words advancing and retreating.

Advancing movements involve a bulging forward of the torso, as if one were becoming the figure-head on the prow of a ship. In advancing, the front surface of the torso becomes convex as if propelling or projecting the body forward.

The reversal of advancing is retreating. Retreating movements involve curving the torso backwards as if one were curling into a deep arm chair, the front surface of the torso becoming concave. Retreating has a withdrawing, retiring quality.

Advancing and retreating shape changes make many functional and expressive actions possible.

1. Advancing shape changes often occur in locomotion: running, leaping to catch a ball; jumping across a ditch; and so on. Advancing might also occur in reaching for a dish on a high shelf or making a grab for a brass ring on a carousel.

2. Leaning forward as if to get a longer view, reaching to shake someone's hand, pressing through a crowd and projecting oneself off a chair are examples of expressive actions in which advancing might occur.

3. Some functional actions in which retreating might occur are the following: crouching to make a racing dive,

relaxing backwards against the curve of the bathtub; waiting for a serve behind the baseline of the tennis court; and curling over while pulling something out of a hot oven.

4. Recoiling in fear, making room for someone to sit in your lap, curling backwards in a chair as if to withdraw from a problem and taking a step backwards in surprise are examples of expressive actions which might involve retreating.

SHAPING IN THE WHEEL PLANE — ITS MEANING

Integrated movements in the wheel plane reveal an anticipatory decision-making style. The anticipatory manager has a natural appreciation as to what is going to result from an action being taken. He is expectantly forward-looking, ready to go on or to drop back as the

Shaping in the wheel plane reveals an anticipatory action motivation.

action develops, this felt sense being expressed physically by shaping in the wheel plane. These shape changes alter one's momentary position, projecting one forward or pulling one back, giving scope for a progression of events. The physical tendency to create sagittal, curving wheel plane shapes reveals a need to act in an anticipatory manner.

SUMMARY

By visualising the moving body surrounded by a kinesphere of space which is trisected by three rectangular planes, we are able to map the ever-changing sculptures created by the moving body. These vanishing concave and convex shapes reveal particular kinds of perspective-oriented action motivations. These correlations are shown in the table below.

Shaping in the ...		*Action motivation*
Table plane (enclosing ⟷ spreading)	reveals	Exploratory style
Door plane (descending ⟷ rising)	reveals	Evaluative style
Wheel plane (retreating ⟷ advancing)	reveals	Anticipatory style

CHAPTER 9

Putting It All Together

We have now briefly surveyed the elements which comprise the movement clusters which make up non-verbal communication. These elements are arranged in three levels or views from which movement can be studied: the body level; the dynamic level; and the sculptural level. From these three levels can be drawn various elements which are relevant to Action Profiling.

BODY PART ACTIVATION AND USAGE

Posture/gesture merger or integrated movement.

DYNAMIC QUALITIES OF EFFORT

1. Focus.
2. Pressure.
3. Pace.
4. Tension flow.

KINETIC SCULPTURE (SHAPING)

1. Shaping in the table plane.
2. Shaping in the door plane.
3. Shaping in the wheel plane.
4. Shape flow.

When a Profile is made, the interviewer/observer attempts, during a two hour interview, to discover those movement patterns which reveal the unique action motivation of the manager being interviewed. The richness and complexity of these movement patterns vary considerably from person to person. Some patterns are bold and obvious while others are subtle and elusive and may require terrific concentration before they can be pinpointed.

Above all, there are no rules. Although the movement elements which have been discussed are universal, the rhythm, phrasing and coordination with which they appear in everyday movements are individual. Each person's pattern of integrated movement is unique.

The following is a movement portrait of one individual. It is included to illustrate how the physical rhythms in conversational behaviour reveal action motivation and movement style.

CASE STUDY

The interviewee in this case is an animated young woman in her early thirties. She works as a personnel director in a large organisation, with responsibility for hiring workers according to clearly defined job specifications. In addition, she runs company training seminars, often working with large groups of employees.

Slender and of moderate height, she sits with her legs crossed at the knee, slumping slightly through her lower back. Her hands rest in her lap. From here they suddenly fly up to make a precise pointing gesture in front of her as she talks. These short choppy phrases occur on more than sixty occasions. From a resting position in her lap her hands and forearms explode into quick jabbing actions, often accompanied by head nods. The hands then return to her lap and there is a moment of quiet before another short burst of activity recurs. Many of these sudden, precise jabbing actions are posture/ gesture mergers, the movement elements being the dynamic qualities of directing and accelerating.

Occasionally the jabbing action becomes more

forceful as increasing pressure is also integrated. At these times the whole texture of her posture changes and she appears to be pressing down against the seat of the chair for emphasis. The forceful movements, however, occur only about twenty-five times during the interview. Sometimes she inclines her head towards the interviewer, leaning forward eagerly in the chair as her hand excitedly chops the air in front of her. In these phrases, which occur twenty-eight times, an advancing posture merges with an advancing gesture.

Often, too, her forearms swing outwards, creating flat arcs in the table plane. Many of these movements are merely gestures, but on twenty-five occasions the chest and legs become involved. A spreading gesture in the arm merges into a spreading posture as the whole body appears to widen.

There is, of course, greater variation in her movement pattern than that described here — these are just some of the key features. A more detailed tabulation of the types of integrated movement which occurred during the interview is shown below.

Movement elements		Frequency of occurrence		
Focus	directing	48	= 62	25%
	indirecting	14		
Table plane	enclosing	12	= 37	15%
	spreading	25		
Pressure	increasing pressure	25	= 30	12%
	decreasing pressure	5		
Door plane	descending	2	= 8	3%
	rising	6		
Pace	accelerating	60	= 75	30%
	decelerating	15		
Wheel plane	retreating	10	= 38	15%
	advancing	28		
Total no. of observations			250 = 100%	

Investigating	25%
ATTENTION	
Exploring	15%
Determining	12%
INTENTION	
Evaluating	3%
Timing	
COMMITMENT	30%
Anticipating	15%

*An example of
an Action Profile.*

When the movement observations are tabulated we see that this interviewee is high in timing and investigating, with moderate strength in exploring and anticipating. She is low in determining and evaluating.

Her approach to decision-making could be summarised in the following way. First she acts, then she doubles back for more information, checks for alternatives and then considers results. Justifying her intentions (determining) and realistically evaluating priorities (evaluating) play minor roles in her decision-making and are often skipped altogether.

These interpretations have been drawn from observing the frequency of occurrence of various dynamic and sculptural elements of motion. However, as we have seen in this illustration, sometimes several factors cluster simultaneously in a single posture/gesture merger. This individual, for instance, often blends two dynamic elements in one action, as in the jabbing posture/gesture mergers which combine directing and accelerating or the rapid postural shifts which combine accelerating with the sculptural element of advancing.

The next chapter introduces other conclusions about an individual's action motivation which can be gleaned from the way in which dynamic elements and shaping elements combine.

CHAPTER 10

Dynamism: Its Kinetic Structure

Perceiving movement as it changes is much like watching waves wash over a beach. As the surf slides across the sand the water turns translucent, revealing bits of shell and pebbles being tumbled about, but even as one reaches to catch a bit of shell, the surf retreats, slipping out to sea and sucking the flotsam with it.

Being able to identify correctly a momentary variation in energy or a vanishing shape is like trying to catch a shell tumbling in the surf. It is not easy, but it is these very observations, evanescent as they are, which form the basis of the Action Profile.

An Action Profile is constructed during a two-to-three hour business interview. The person making the Profile may conduct the interview himself, or may have someone else do the interviewing. It is important to create an atmosphere in which the interviewee is both relaxed about and engaged by the questioning. While the Profiler does rely on verbal information for interpreting and counselling, the Profile itself is based on movement data.

During such an interview a skilled Profiler will be able to identify and record 200–250 incidences of integrated effort or shape change. As we have seen in the previous chapter, these recorded identifications can be used to create percentages based on the frequency of occurrence of an element relative to the total number of observations taken. From this an Action Profile can be constructed. For example (using the same case study), let us say that out of 250 observations one is able to identify 25 incidences of increasing pressure and 5 incidences of decreasing pressure, giving a total of 30 incidences in all of pressure variation. When we divide this by the total number of observations taken (250) we see that pressure variation occurred about 12 per cent of the time. Pressure variation reveals a determined decision-making style, and therefore we can say that determining plays a weak role in the unique composition of the subject's action motivation.

We have been using the term "number of incidences" rather than "number of integrated movements" for an important reason, since a single posture/gesture merger may be recorded more than once if more than one movement quality is integrated. If we return to our seaside analogy, one shell tossing in the surf may be lavender, another beige and lavender, while a third is beige, lavender and pink. Similarly, two or three qualities of effort or shaping may blend together in a single posture/gesture merger, and this blending of qualities gives movement a distinctly different look and meaning.

For instance, the interviewee might tap the table pointedly with a gentle but immutable insistence. If we analyse this tapping we would find that the effort elements of directing, decreasing pressure and accelerating are blended into one movement. These elements correspond respectively with the action motivations of investigating, determining and timing. When tapping, this interviewee is assertively attending, intending and committing, all at once.

Similarly, an interviewee could propel himself forward, arching his back and opening his arms expansively. If we analyse the composition of this integrated movement we would discover a combination of advancing and spreading. These shaping elements correspond respectively with anticipating and exploring. This interviewee is simultaneously gaining perspective about committing and attending.

The two examples above, one composed of blended dynamic elements, the other of combined shape elements, pave the way to a new understanding of dynamism in managerial decision-making. They show that it is possible to be attending to one decision, forming intentions about a second and making a commitment on a third. The appearance of dynamic blends, like the tapping action, or of shaping combinations, like the advancing and spreading motion, indicate the simultaneous involvement of the mover in more than one cycle or stage of decision-making. The frequency of occurrence of kinetic combinations gives a rough measure of the intensity of a person's initiative or dynamism.

Dynamism, from an Action Profile point of view, represents the number of non-routine cycles of decision-making that a person can handle simultaneously. The key word here is *non-routine* — the dynamism measured by the Profile does not include routine decision-making. With training and experience a number of seemingly decisive actions can be implemented almost automatically, without research or evaluation. Routine decisions are really made by rote. Only those novel decisions which require real preliminary consideration and careful control of timing are measured as dynamism in the Action Profile.

Dynamism, which is represented in the Profile by a sliding scale of 1–10, has the following implications in management behaviour. An individual with low dynamism (1–5) will be careful not to undertake too many decision-making processes at a given time. This individual will tend to make fewer decisions at a time and will be reluctant to initiate another decision-making cycle until he completes most of the projects on hand. However, an individual with moderate to high dynamism (5–10) will be willing to take on more decisions at once, being able to handle many cycles simultaneously. He will be able to have perhaps two projects on the back burners and two more at full boil without feeling overloaded.

However, high dynamism does not guarantee that an executive actually gets more done or is more effective. While the highly dynamic manager is willing to tackle a lot, the effectiveness of his performance depends on his skill and intelligence as well as how the job is structured. High dynamism is an attribute in a skilled executive who has found his niche and developed a successful work strategy. However, a less dynamic executive can also be extremely effective provided he is intelligent, skilled and that care is taken to place him in the right job and to prevent him from becoming overloaded.

CHAPTER 11

Harmony in Motion

We have described various blends of qualities of effort and blends of change of shape, and we have discussed how these blends indicate the level of an individual's dynamism. But what does it mean when a dynamic change and a shape change are integrated in the same movement?

In the course of his researches on movement Rudolf Laban came to feel that there were natural harmonic relationships between certain spatial directions and dynamic qualities. For instance, *directing*, with its linear, unswerving approach, seemed linked to a narrowing of the horizon brought about by *enclosing*. *Indirecting*, with its more curvaceous, roundabout approach, seemed connected with *spreading* and a spanning of the horizon. *Increasing pressure* seemed to correlate with *descending* and going with the pull of gravity, while *decreasing pressure* went with shapes curving upwards which defy gravity by *rising*. *Accelerating* seemed to relate to *retreating*, as in the reflex response of pulling back from danger, while *decelerating* was linked with *advancing*, as in the cautious forward creep of an animal about to pounce.

It is impossible to say whether Laban made these correlations based on direct observation, intuition or some combination of the two. However, Warren Lamb and Pamela Ramsden have tested Laban's theory of

*There are naturally occurring harmonic relationships between certain
spatial directions and certain dynamic qualities.*

harmonic movements in the observations they have
taken during interviews. They have been able to
determine that harmonic and dissonant couplings of
dynamic qualities with qualities of shape do indeed
create distinctive atmospheres of communication which

are related to each phase of decision-making. These
couplings are shown in the table below.

Movement parameters of interactional style

Harmonic pairings

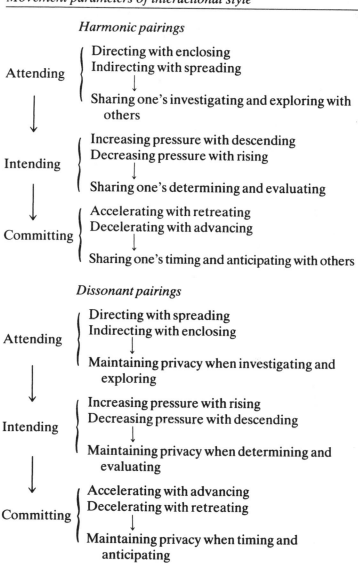

Attending
⟨
Directing with enclosing
Indirecting with spreading
↓
Sharing one's investigating and exploring with
  others
⟩

Intending
⟨
Increasing pressure with descending
Decreasing pressure with rising
↓
Sharing one's determining and evaluating
⟩

Committing
⟨
Accelerating with retreating
Decelerating with advancing
↓
Sharing one's timing and anticipating with others
⟩

Dissonant pairings

Attending
⟨
Directing with spreading
Indirecting with enclosing
↓
Maintaining privacy when investigating and
  exploring
⟩

Intending
⟨
Increasing pressure with rising
Decreasing pressure with descending
↓
Maintaining privacy when determining and
  evaluating
⟩

Committing
⟨
Accelerating with advancing
Decelerating with retreating
↓
Maintaining privacy when timing and
  anticipating
⟩

Based on the movement observations taken during the interview, it is possible to compute the potential for matching and mis-matching elements of effort and shape. This potential harmony or dissonance is realised when the individual is engaged in making decisions with others. Part 3 looks at the interactional implications of these silent accords and discords.

PART THREE
*Top Team Planning —
The Profile in Action
and Interaction*

CHAPTER 12

Interaction

The pressures of decision-making call for cooperative team action and cohesive leadership at the top. It is critical, therefore, that the unique interactional styles of senior staff members mesh in constructive ways. This, alas, is too often not the case: different interactional needs can create politically destructive conflicts within a team. However, the understanding of interaction provided by movement study can help to prevent this.

Let us clarify what we mean by the term interaction. Interaction can be defined as all manner of acting and reacting with others when engaged in a decision-making process. Action Profiler Pamela Ramsden has delineated three distinct interactive modes.

1. An individual can have the need to share decision-making with others, to work interdependently.
2. A person can have the need to make decisions independently, to keep others out of the process.
3. One can be neutral, neither actively including nor excluding others from the decision-making process.

These distinctive interactive styles each have their own felt sense relative to the stage of decision-making in which the individual is involved.

ATTENTION PHASE STYLES OF INTERACTION

For example, let us consider an individual who is motivated to share the attention phase activities of

91

Different interactive needs can create conflict within a management team.

investigating and exploring. This person wants to contribute information and ideas to his colleagues and welcomes thoughts and feedback from them. He often plays a harmonising and sympathising role in a meeting, making co-workers feel that they are genuinely listened to and heeded. He encourages others to investigate and explore with him, creating an atmosphere where mutual exchange of information can take place.

The private attender, on the other hand, prefers to conduct investigations and explorations alone. He carries out research as if he were underwater and the rest of the staff were above water, only surfacing from time to time in order to report formally the results of his information gathering. It is only at this point that his colleagues are invited to comment on the findings, but he resists their attempts to build upon his research or to engage actively in the sharing and exchange of ideas. Instead, he needs to submerge again, to consider their comments in private.

INTENTION PHASE STYLES OF INTERACTION

A different interactional style is seen in the individual who is motivated to share the intention phase activities of determining and evaluating. This person needs to involve others in the amassing of evidence and the development of priorities to support his side of an issue. In a meeting he takes on the role of influencing and convincing colleagues. Highly persuasive, he can help the group reach a consensus.

The independent intender, on the other hand, again prefers to do his determining and evaluating underwater, in isolation. He surfaces to make a formal statement on an issue, yet he invests little energy in rallying others to support this point of view. While his colleagues are welcome to state their opinions, they often find it difficult to involve this independent character in a debate, to pressurise or influence him. Colleagues sense that he is guided by a private sense of conviction, yet they are excluded from participation in this purposeful quest.

COMMITMENT PHASE STYLES OF INTERACTION

Yet another interactional style is demonstrated by the individual who is motivated to share the commitment phase activities of timing and anticipating with others. This individual creates an atmosphere in which activities are speeded up or delayed, where past developments are recalled and the results of current projects jointly anticipated. The sharing committer engenders in colleagues an awareness of the timing and the objectives of the task at hand. Colleagues working with him gain an understanding of the organisational priorities of the timetable, the goal of the project and their own roles and schedules in its implementation.

The independent committer wants to handle such a task on his own, needing to anticipate it and organise its timing privately. Because of this, the independent committer inadvertently creates a secretive atmosphere around himself, and colleagues may feel that he is precipitating action and pursuing objectives behind their backs. When involved in implementing a project with others the private committer may leave his co-workers in the dark as to what the timetable and objectives really are.

NEUTRAL INTERACTION

Some interactions involve neither actively sharing nor actively creating a "hands off" atmosphere. Many are polite, noncommittal interchanges which are rather neutral in tone, and the potential for this kind of interaction is always present in each phase of the action process.

In a neutral interaction the individual is motivated neither to draw people into his activity nor to actively maintain his independence. In this type of interaction the person's energy is "on display". His attitude says "I'm attending, intending or committing. Take it or leave it." In short, in a neutral interaction the manager's energy is available to the interactional initiatives of others. This means that the person who is in a neutral mood can fit in readily with whatever interactive or individual line of approach others wish to create. This, naturally, leads to a tolerance of other people's interactive needs. However, a person who is mostly interactively neutral will take little personal initiative in establishing the tone of his dealings with others and may sometimes be perceived as insensitive.

VERSATILE INTERACTION

Some individuals have a great deal of potential versatility in the kinds of interactions they can structure with others. These people are motivated both to share their decision-making and to make decisions privately. This means that such individuals have a need to work with and through their colleagues as well as needing the scope to work alone. They can positively and constructively include others in gathering information, resolving policy, scheduling activities and setting goals, but they can also carry on the activities of attending, intending or committing by themselves.

This sometimes-sharing/sometimes-private interactive style will manifest itself differently from day to day and from situation to situation. In fact, a versatile individual can probably control an interaction, choosing when and with whom he will share and when and with whom he will remain private. This on/off quality may make him appear unpredictable to colleagues, but it can also be the basis for genuine tolerance of the interactive needs of co-workers.

INTERACTION IS A TWO-WAY STREET

Interaction is a two-way street; it depends upon the needs of the moment and the interactive styles of the two (or more) people involved. Research carried out by Pamela Ramsden suggests that there is nothing pre-ordained about interaction. While the Profile represents tendencies or preferences, every individual has considerable scope to vary his interactive behaviour within each phase and from phase to phase.

However, the potential for variation does not mean that an individual *will* be flexible or sensitive in his dealings with colleagues. An individual's manner of working with others is often emotionally highly charged; a clash in interactive styles, even momentarily, causes duress, just as a mesh of styles produces a pleasant sense of rapport.

The following scenarios were developed by Pamela Ramsden, based on her interviews with senior managers and her observations of senior teams in action. These scenarios portray some of the possible feelings that may arise from various matches and mismatches in interactive style.

How i feel towards another when i am in the attending phase

1. When we are both sharing attention-phase activities, I feel understood, sparked by a mutual sense

of interest and discovery. As we clarify points and explore tangents, I feel that I am being heeded. I am able to get my ideas across easily.

2. When both of us are attending, but I want to share and he wants to remain private, I sense that he is not paying attention or listening to me. I feel misunderstood.

3. When I am sharing attention, but he is sharing intention, I feel that I am unable to get a word in edgewise. I feel I am being bulldozed and forced to argue my points.

4. When I am sharing attention, but he is sharing commitment, I feel that I am being rushed into making a decision. I feel unable to get a look at the facts or to establish priorities.

5. When I have moved on to sharing either intention or commitment, but he is still sharing attention, I feel irritated by irrelevancies, impatient and eager to move on to getting things on a more definite level and more action-oriented. His attempts to communicate are preventing my getting a grip on things and making a decision. I want to escape.

6. When both of us are privately attending, but we are forced by circumstances to cooperate, I feel as though we are just informing one another of the facts mechanically. I would much rather be doing my own thing.

HOW I FEEL TOWARDS ANOTHER WHEN I AM IN THE INTENDING PHASE

1. When we are both sharing intention phase activities I feel challenged. I feel urged to take a stand on the issues, and confident of saying what I mean with no nonsense. I feel we are coming to grips with the problem and I am very sure of the position we are taking.

2. When both of us are intending, but I want to share

and he wants to remain private, I feel unable to come to grips with the problem. I am unable to say what I mean and am confused as to what our position really is.

3. When I am sharing intending but he is sharing attending, I feel I am being given more information than I need. His communicating is preventing my getting a grip on the issues at hand.

4. When I am sharing intending but he is sharing committing, I feel as if I am being put on the spot. I sense I am being rushed into action before I have established what ought to be done.

5. When I have moved on to sharing either attention or commitment, but he is still sharing intention, I feel I am not being listened to nor am I able to get things moving fast enough. I feel he is putting pressure on me to agree with his views. I feel bulldozed and want to escape.

6. When both of us are privately intending, but we are forced by the circumstances to cooperate, I feel we are just bemusing each other with hollow-sounding statements of intent. I would much rather pursue my private crusade.

HOW I FEEL TOWARD ANOTHER WHEN I AM IN THE COMMITTING PHASE

1. When we are both sharing commitment phase activities I experience an exhilarating sense of pace. I feel we are taking moment-to-moment decisions with urgency or calm precision while alerting ourselves to the next steps. I feel we are able to get things moving.

2. When both of us are committing, but I want to share and he wants to remain private, I feel I am not being alerted to what is happening. I feel unable to get things moving.

3. When I am sharing commitment, but he is sharing attention I feel unable to get anything decided. He is

boring me with too much waffle when all I want to do is get the ball rolling.

4. When I am sharing commitment but he is sharing intention I feel unable to get things moving fast enough. I feel I have to argue my points in order to prevent my being bulldozed.

5. When I have moved to sharing attention or intention but he is still sharing commitment I want to slow down, to look into the facts properly and to establish what ought to be done. I feel uncomfortable with the pace he is setting and I want to escape.

6. When both of us are privately committing, but are forced by circumstances to cooperate, I feel that we are making a plan of action mechanically, forcing ourselves to stay in step. I would prefer to march to the beat of my own drum.

"THE MAN WHO CRIED WOLF" REVISITED

When individuals make decisions in very different ways the possibility of conflict is always there. When these individuals have no shared interactive mode the probability that they will misunderstand each other increases. Such a situation occurred in the tale of the man who cried wolf which was given in Chapter 1. In the story Ernest Dobson, a professional financial manager, finds himself out of step with the creative, impetuous artists who run the company for which he works.

Dobson's major channel of interaction is through sharing the intention phase activities of determining and evaluating, while the rest of the management team shares the activities of either attending or committing. This makes Dobson the odd man out. He feels irritated with what to him are the wild irrelevancies which his colleagues discuss with great zest, he is panicked by the feeling that they rush headlong into decisions and he feels, rightly so, that his colleagues actually prevent the company from establishing a clear policy and getting to grips with critical issues.

On the other hand, Dobson's colleagues feel he interferes with their open-ended discussions and thwarts their ability to take timely and decisive action. Dobson appears to badger them, while all they want to do is escape from his attempts to share his intentions.

Ultimately they succeed in making Dobson feel as if he is standing "on a soap box, haranguing deaf people". While Dobson supplies certain motivations which are missing from the team as a whole, his contribution is foiled because he is unable to establish real interaction. The company suffers in the process.

This invented fable is an example of the kind of interactive mismatch which can easily develop into destructive conflict. However, this need not necessarily be the case. Indeed the odd man out can be an asset to a team if they understand the nature of his contribution and have constructive and acceptable ways to turn on and turn off the maverick's input. Unfortunately this is not easy to achieve because of the nature of interaction itself.

Research on non-verbal communication indicates that human interaction is grounded in subtle but powerful physical behaviours, some of which are so subtle that they can only be perceived in very painstaking, frame-by-frame analyses of films. Yet all of us are able to perceive these physical signs intuitively, in that they create the complex felt sense we have of another person. A shift in a relationship may not be seen but it will be felt, either positively or negatively.

The very subtlety of the physical behaviour in which interaction is grounded, and the fact that most of us perceive these behaviours only subliminally, has contributed to the "mystifying" of human interactions.

One is inexplicably "on the same wave length" with another, "the vibrations are good", or you "just can't get it together", you "aren't in sync". While such phrases aptly capture the emotional ramifications of interactive matches and mismatches, they do little to improve the ability to work alongside someone else.

While Action Profiling cannot begin to explain human interaction completely, it does provide a terminology for understanding some of the behaviour which relates to decision-making. This understanding can then be used to demystify what goes on in the executive offices of a company and, more importantly, to improve the cohesion and effectiveness of the senior team.

SUMMARY

This discussion of interaction completes our survey of the elements of decision-making style which are revealed by Action Profiling. We can sum up this survey as follows.

1. Decision-making is conceptualised as a three-stage process, beginning with giving attention to the project, followed by forming an intention to act and concluded by making a commitment and actually implementing a decision.

2. Warren Lamb has found that each individual will take either an assertive or a perspective oriented approach to these three stages of action, and these approaches comprise the six basic action motivations or decision-making styles. These styles are as follows: investigative; exploratory; determined; evaluative; time-keeping; anticipatory.

3. Pamela Ramsden has delineated various interaction styles which relate to this decision-making process: sharing or remaining private in the attention phase; sharing or remaining private in the intention

phase; and sharing or remaining private in the commitment phase, being either neutral or versatile. All these produce different manners of working with others and can create feelings of rapport or conflict.

4. Identifying, adaptability and dynamism complete the elements which comprise an Action Profile.

All these elements are shown below. The following chapter will show how Warren Lamb and his associates have used the Action Profile within actual companies.

THE FRAMEWORK OF MANAGEMENT STYLE

ATTENDING

	Assertion	*Perspective*
Individual	Investigating: probing, scanning and classifying information within a prescribed area. Outcome: systematic research, establishing methods and defining standards.	Exploring: broadening scope, uncovering, encompassing and perceiving information from many areas. Outcome: creative brainstorming, discovering alternatives.
Interactive	Sharing attending: giving genuine attention to others, listening to them and drawing them out; inviting them to share in probing the existing situation and/or bringing in new aspects for attention; sharing one's own process of investigation and exploration.	
	Private attending: investigating and exploring independently; results are reported; others are not invited into the process of gathering information.	
	Neutral attending: depending on the initiatives of others to catalyse interaction.	
	Versatile attending: sharing is switched on and off; interdependent and independent.	

INTENDING

	Assertion	*Perspective*
Individual	Determining: affirming purpose, building resolve, forging conviction, justifying intent. Outcome: persisting against odds, maintaining strength of will.	Evaluating: gauging pros and cons, sizing up the issues, perceiving proportion. Outcome: clarifying intentions, realistically appraising facts and proposals.

Interactive Sharing intending: making a positive demonstration, declaring intentions, influencing, persuading, emphasising, insisting, resisting and inviting others to do likewise; sharing one's own process of determining and evaluating.

Private intending: determining and evaluating independently; stating beliefs; others are not invited into the process of forging and shaping resolve.

Neutral intending: depending on the initiatives of others to catalyse interaction.

Versatile intending: sharing is switched on and off; interdependent and independent.

COMMITTING

	Assertion	*Perspective*
Individual	Timing: pacing implementation, sensing the moment-by-moment timing of action. Outcome: adjusting time priorities for opportune implementation.	Anticipating: perceiving the developing stages of action and sensing the consequences of each stage. Outcome: setting goals, measuring progress and updating plans.

Interactive Sharing committing: on the spot organising of
people; creating a sense of urgency or slowing
down the pace; spurring people on or delaying
activity with awareness of the implications of action
and objectives; developing the action and inviting
others to do the same; sharing one's own process of
timing and anticipating.

Private committing: timing and anticipating
independently; not including others in staging
or developing action.

Neutral committing: depending on the initiatives
of others to catalyse interaction.

Versatile committing: sharing is switched on and
off; interdependent and independent.

ADDITIONAL FACTORS

Dynamism: the number of novel or non-routine
cycles of decision-making a person will initiate
simultaneously.

Adaptability: an individual's willingness to alter
his most basic attitudes to fit in with a changing
situation.

Identifying: the person's response quotient, the
readiness to respond and spontaneously associate
self with centres of activity in the company.

CHAPTER 13

Team Building: Case Histories

"... equilibrium is never complete stability or a standstill, but the result of two contrasting qualities of mobility."

Rudolf Laban

When Action Profiling is introduced to a company the consultant's goal is to help establish motivational equilibrium within the senior staff. In order to do this each of the six basic action motivations must be represented, i.e. there must be someone who is highly investigative, someone who is highly exploratory, someone who is highly determined, someone who is highly evaluative, someone who is very aware of timing, and someone who is highly anticipatory. Moreover, there must be a common channel of interaction between team members to insure that each individual's unique contribution will be recognised and understood. This kind of motivational blend helps to produce team balance.

This concept of team balance applies movement thinking to management. As Laban points out in the quotation above, balance is not static. Rather, real balance results from contrasting actions. Thus the goal of top team planning is to build a senior team which can cope with all the changing demands of managing in a real world of change. This means that senior managers who

*Contrasting but complementary Action Profiles keep senior
management teams in balance.*

are constantly taking action should be acting in
contrasting but complementary ways. Too much
emphasis on any single action motivation, or too little,
can be disastrous for a company. Top team planning
using Action Profiling aims to guard against this.

A top team planning assignment consists of several
steps. First the top team must be defined and individual
profiles drawn for each member. Team members will
then be counselled individually or in pairs about their
profiles in order to help each person gain insight about
his decision-making style. From these individual profiles
an Action Profile team analysis is done. A team profile is
created by averaging individual scores in each area, this
composite profile then being used to analyse team
strengths and weaknesses.

At this point the application of the team analysis is
tailored to the needs and atmosphere of the company.
The goal is to help the team function better. This can be
accomplished in several ways: through enhancing the
team's awareness of its own strengths and weaknesses;
through redefining roles and creating special project
groups utilising those managers whose motivations are
appropriate to the task; through learning techniques to

compensate for weaknesses; and through using changes in staff to improve team balance.

The stories that follow are actual histories of different teams which have been Profiled. Some of the stories have happy endings, some not, but all illustrate principles of team balance or imbalance and show how the action motivations of the senior team critically affect the function and profitability of a company.

ATTENTION	Investigating	8%
	Exploring	2%
	Determining	12%
INTENTION		
	Evaluating	18%
	Timing	35%
COMMITMENT		
	Anticipating	25%

The wheeler–dealers. Action Profile of the managing director.

ATTENTION	Investigating	15%
	Exploring	10%
INTENTION	Determining	13%
	Evaluating	18%
COMMITMENT	Timing	23%
	Anticipating	21%

The wheeler–dealers. Team Profile.

THE WHEELER–DEALERS

The simplified profile shown below belongs to the managing director of a company which processed raw goods. As his Profile indicates, he is extremely low in attending (a mere 10 per cent) and extremely high in committing (a remarkable 60 per cent). The man was, in fact, something of a wheeler–dealer. As the managing director he engaged in the impulsive buying and selling of companies, often executing actions with little prior information or consideration.

This impetuous decisive streak would often appear during advising sessions with the Action Profile consultant. The consultant found that no sooner would he make a recommendation than the managing director would be on the phone executing the consultant's suggestion.

The managing director had built up a management team which was composed of wheeler-dealers like himself, as the team profile indicates. This team profile was composed by averaging the individual scores of the nine senior people. Of these, the two men who were divisional managing directors had profiles that were almost identical with that of the managing director. Of the six other team members only one was high in attending, and he was neither heeded nor valued by his colleagues.

This lopsided emphasis on commitment, coupled with weak attending motivation, meant that the team would invariably leap before they looked. They continually executed action without proper preparation or sufficient information and as a result they kept making errors, decisions would go awry and projects would misfire.

The team was able to get over a lot of these mistakes. Being high committers, they could find short-term solutions through quick action by merely making adjustments in the course of projects they were already embarked upon. However, to stop action altogether, to go back to the drawing board, to rethink or to try a new approach (all attending activities) were solutions that never occurred to them.

Ultimately a fraud was uncovered in the company. This was a slip that not even quick action could repair, and during the upheaval that followed this discovery the managing director was ousted by the chairman of the board — the team had become so out of balance that it finally toppled itself.

THE WAVERERS

The team in this case history managed a small architectural firm. The firm was started by the owner, who gradually added four other people as partners. These partners were all selected through the "contact network" and appointed informally. As so often happens when this is the case, the people who joined the team were similar. When the Action Profile consultant was called in she found that the team had got itself out of balance. Nevertheless, the company was doing well financially.

There was only one fly in the ointment, and this problem had to do with interaction. The Action Profile consultant found that team members were prone to misunderstand each other, often finding themselves at cross-purposes. When this happened small problems became large problems and the group experienced considerable interpersonal friction.

For example, at one time the team thought they might move their offices. Each member of the team had his or her own opinion as to what kind of office the company needed and where that office should be, e.g. the owner kept trooping the other partners out to look at country mansions. Without directly confronting the issue — that they did not want to move to the country — the other team members found something wrong with each of these mansions and thus had legitimate reasons not to take any of them. This pattern continued. Then one day one of the partners found a suitable office in the city while at the same time the owner found a new country office. This time, when the team trooped out to look at the country office, they could find nothing wrong with it. It was as suitable as the city office.

Being faced with two equally viable opportunities threw the team into an uproar. Up to this point they had been acting individually without a shared sense of what was important. Now the situation demanded they share their priorities in order to reach some kind of consensus and make a decision. A great deal of friction developed as the team struggled with what should have been a comparatively simple problem.

Investigating	22%
ATTENTION	
Exploring	17%
Determining	13%
INTENTION	
Evaluating	13%
Timing	23%
COMMITMENT	
Anticipating	12%

The waverers. Team Profile.

A look at the team profile reveals why the team got itself into these hassles. It shows the firm to be particularly strong in investigating and timing, with moderate strength in exploring. This combination of strengths made the team quick on their feet, analytical, inventive; they were ready to put their knowledge to work and were precise and methodical in timing the implementation of their ideas. Unfortunately, however, they were low in determining and evaluating, which meant that the intention stage was the weak link for them; they tended, as a group, to skip the processes of affirming the purpose of actions, sizing up issues and setting priorities for themselves.

These problems were exacerbated by the interaction pattern of the team in the intention area. As the chart reveals, the team is more likely to be private about their intentions than to share them. There is also a tendency, particularly with Partners 3 and 4, for the team to be neutral, i.e. for each of them to wait for someone else to initiate interaction.

The Action Profile consultant felt that it was this tendency to be private or neutral about intentions that was creating the interpersonal friction within the team. Her aim in working with the team was to make them

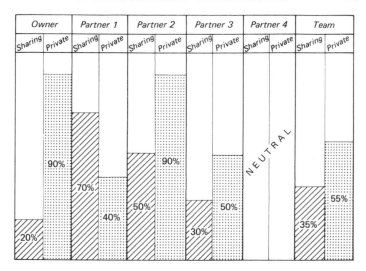

Owner		Partner 1		Partner 2		Partner 3		Partner 4		Team	
Sharing	Private	Sharing	Private	Sharing	Private	Sharing	Private	Sharing	Private	Sharing	Private

The waverers. Team interaction in the intention phase.
A percentage indicates the potential *for sharing or witholding in*
this stage of decision-making.

sensitive to those situations in which friction was likely to develop and to help them find ways of avoiding this.

As a first step towards this goal she had periodic meetings with the team. Here individual profiles and the team profile were reviewed in the light of the current activities of the company, and ways of applying team action motivations were suggested. In particular the consultant used these sessions to urge the team to be alert to their weakness in intention and their tendency to skip over this stage when making decisions. Because the consultant herself was strong in intention her input bolstered the team, helping them to clarify issues and set priorities. What the consultant was really doing in these meetings was helping the team to maintain an awareness of the Profile and to relate it to current actions of the firm.

Secondly, she guided the team in finding ways of developing a mutually shared sense of purpose. Because team members had independent views of the goals of the various activities of the firm they had difficulty measuring company performance realistically. As a result they tended to undervalue their accomplishments. Once the consultant had made team members aware of this weakness they were able to establish their own creative method for coping with it. Their solution was to have a champagne celebration every time they got a new client. This somewhat whimsical strategy did make them more aware of their successes and also furthered their cohesion as a team.

Because of low intention and neutral/private interaction in that area the team found it particularly difficult to maintain a mutual sense of purpose in the face of hardships or setbacks. When they were not able to translate their ideas into action immediately they became disheartened. This could also happen when an action did not go the way they intended, and in this case the problem of morale was complicated by the fact that each of the five partners could have a different view of the purpose of the action. Faced with an obstacle, they were not able to rally themselves around a flag of common purpose. Consequently, when a project went badly the team tended to fall apart and, as the group splintered, friction would develop.

Again, using insight gained from the team analysis, the group was able to formulate an inventive solution. They began to have what they called celebration weekends. During these weekends they would go away as a group to various resort areas. These weekend retreats helped them to establish themselves as a group away from the office and also provided them with time to discuss business issues and company goals informally.

After several years of working with the consultant the team discontinued their periodic meetings with her. Since that time they have again begun to experience interpersonal conflict. Recently when the owner tried to set up a celebration weekend he was unable to do so.

The continuing problems of this team indicate the liability of relying on a technique to compensate for the gap in action motivation in intention, which was partially filled by the Action Profiler. Without the constant reinforcement provided by the consultant the team just stopped using the technique they had developed, and their problems returned.

A more long-lasting solution of course would be for this team to recruit a partner who is strong in intention and has the capacity to share. The next case history shows how another company employed this kind of strategy to overcome a team imbalance.

THE PROCRASTINATORS

The following case history represents another team which was out of balance, but its lopsidedness takes a different form to that of the previous team.

Investigating	19%
ATTENTION	
Exploring	20%
Determining	19%
INTENTION	
Evaluating	8%
Timing	10%
COMMITMENT	
Anticipating	24%

The procrastinators.
Team Profile.

The team profile belongs to a senior team of four people who were running an industrial textile company which was part of a larger group. At the time that the team was Profiled the company had been making a loss for nine years and the top team did not seem to be able to turn the company around financially. The four directors were frustrated as a group and frustrated with each other.

In addition the consultant found that there was an amazing amount of self-deception amongst team members. The managers seemed to be able to rationalise their poor performance by adopting an attitude of "Things will go on. You can't do it all at once. We'll get it right *some* day."

A closer look at the team profile provides insight into how this atmosphere came into being. The team had two particular weaknesses; they were extremely low in timing and they were also low in evaluating.

The weakness in timing meant that they simply did not take enough action. The team tended to concentrate its energies in the preliminary stages of decision-making and were not assertive enough about implementing the ideas that were arrived at. Opportunities to effect a financial turnaround were passed by simply because the team could not mobilise itself swiftly enough.

The weakness in evaluating contributed to the unrealistic attitude the managers had about the company. They were simply not facing up to the issues, they were not owning up to the critical need for action on their parts and they were relying on persistence and wishful thinking to carry them through.

After being in the position for three years without changing the company's financial situation the Managing Director was removed, and the Action Profile consultant was called in again. He helped the parent group find a new managing director with a better awareness of timing and who also had experience in doctoring companies. Profiles of the former managing director and the new managing director are shown together.

What was very significant about the appointment of the new managing director was the effect he had on the team Profile. His strength in timing singlehandedly brought the team average up 5 per cent, making it a moderately strong feature of the team profile.

When the Action Profile consultant visited the company four months after the appointment of the new managing director he found it to be a changed environment. It was clear that the other directors were

Investigating	18%
ATTENTION	
Exploring	36%
Determining **INTENTION**	10%
Evaluating	4%
Timing	14%
COMMITMENT	
Anticipating	18%

The procrastinators. Action Profile of the former managing director.

Investigating **ATTENTION**	22%
Exploring	8%
Determining **INTENTION**	14%
Evaluating	10%
Timing	32%
COMMITMENT	
Anticipating	14%

The procrastinators. Action Profile of the new managing director.

feeling the impact of having a time-keeper in their midst. Decisions seemed to be flying through the air. The company seemed headed for recovery.

In all fairness it must be noted that the previous managing director was extremely high in exploring. Although he had been unable to effect a financial turnaround himself, he had undoubtedly paved the way with innovative preparation. However, it took a time-keeper to capitalise on the groundwork laid by the explorer and to bring it to fruition by mobilising the whole team.

THE ACHIEVERS

The next case history is the story of a highly successful publishing group which was both profitable and efficient. At the time the Action Profile consultant was called in the company had recently switched from being a family owned and run company to being professionally managed. The new senior team consisted of five men, the managing director and the financial, marketing, production and editorial directors, all of whom were recognised as national talents in their fields. At the time the new team took over the company was phasing out of a period of moderate growth and into a period of major reorganisation.

The Action Profile team analysis was suggested by the managing director, who felt intuitively that the team had not yet meshed as a functioning board. The managing director had discovered that when he asked his board what the company strategy was all gave a reply, but implicit in the replies was the unspoken attitude that "It's your job to decide that". While the managing director felt he could make all the strategic decisions for a while, he was worried that, in the long run, he would not have the full commitment of the rest of the board, that they would not "own" his strategic decisions. The need to cultivate greater cohesion among his directors prompted the managing director to turn to Action Profiling.

Investigating	23%
ATTENTION	
Exploring	15%
Determining	19%
INTENTION	
Evaluating	8%
Timing	24%
COMMITMENT	
Anticipating	11%

The achievers. Team Profile.

Subsequently a team profile was made, which bore out the managing director's gut feeling in that it revealed that the group was low in perspective elements (only 34 per cent overall). The team was particularly weak in evaluating (8 per cent) and anticipating (11 per cent). This meant that, although the team tended to be aggressive in its actions, decisions were made without a sense of what the company mission was or what the long-range implications and results of a decision would be.

In the light of this interpretation of the team profile the consultant recommended that the team undertake training in strategic management techniques, and found another consultant who did strategic management training. The Profiler selected this particular consultant because he also happened to be high in perspective motivations. Thus the Profiler felt that not only would he contribute a technique, but also he would transmit to the team the flavour and feel for thinking strategically, since he was strongly motivated in this way himself.

A programme of two-day seminars was initiated over the following year, the first seminar being handled jointly by the Action Profiler and the strategic management trainer. In this seminar the consultants guided team members in studying themselves in action, using video tape for feedback. The second, third and fourth seminars, held at regular intervals with the strategic management consultant, had the team working together on strategy formulation.

When the team had first been counselled on their Action Profiles they had not been able to recognise their strengths and weaknesses very clearly. However, in the course of the seminars on strategy formulation, they began to work together as a decision-making body, and they began to see their strengths and weaknesses in action. For example, in one exercise in strategic thinking they were asked to define what their mission was. This exercise was extremely difficult for them. The only mission they could think of was that they were in business to survive and not to go broke. Their difficulty in carrying out this exercise underscored the weakness in the intention area which had been revealed by the team study, particularly the low level of evaluating. They found that they were not motivated to crystallise what was important to them.

After the year of training in strategic management was completed a further one-day seminar was conducted by the Action Profiler and the strategic management trainer. This seminar emphasised an understanding of the composite Action Profile of the team and included reviewing the individual Action Profiles as well as the team profile, videotaping the team in action and establishing what actions could be taken to optimise team strengths and guard against weaknesses in the light of the newly-developed company strategy. This seminar revealed how much progress had been made towards working as a group. The directors were able to look at the Action Profile team analysis by themselves, and they were able to formulate the following actions.

As a way of coping with low intention they proposed using formal progress and assessment procedures to let the middle management know where the company was going.

To cope with low evaluating and anticipating they proposed several actions. Quantifying objectives and improving measurement of achievement was suggested as a way to clarify what was important (evaluating) and to gauge progress towards goals (anticipating). They also felt they could capitalise on the strengths of the two team members who were relatively strong in anticipating and evaluating — the production director (26 per cent anticipating) and the editorial director (12 per cent evaluating). They proposed listening to these two and using them as "alarm bells".

Because sharing attention was their strongest channel of interaction they proposed having working lunches where they could informally exchange ideas and information.

In the intention area the team tended to be private or neutrally interactive. They were concerned to make sure that an intended action was clear to and agreed by everyone. Consequently they suggested ground rules.

1. Don't assume the obvious.

2. Don't assume that there is negative disagreement.
3. Check that everyone agrees.
4. Paraphrase understanding of the agreement.

The thoroughness with which this team was able to "own" their profiles and to propose ways of using the information is remarkable. The element of high timing in the team profile, coupled with high investigating, undoubtedly motivated them to want to put the information gleaned from the team analysis into action. Moreover, to undergo a year of training in strategy development represented a massive commitment to work together on their weaknesses as a team.

This year of teamwork on an area of difficulty focused the team on their decision-making process. Undoubtedly, it was this year of struggle which made the Profiles real and enabled the team to be so concrete in seeing possible action.

A year and a half from the beginning of the team study the progress made by the team was impressive. But what happened subsequently? Did they follow up their proposed actions?

FOLLOW UP

A follow up study was conducted close to a year after the final team-building seminar was held. The purpose of this study was to assess how effective the introduction of Action Profiling had been. The managing director was questioned about the general effectiveness of Profiling as well as about specific follow through on the actions they proposed to take. The following points were revealed.

Lowest area — intending
The team had been able to follow through with the proposed action relating to this point.

First, they felt they were better able to recognise

decisions which required the enthusiasm and support of the team. They recognised that, if there was to be a lot of independent discretion as to how the decision was to be carried out (commitment phase), then more people had to be involved in agreeing to the idea (intention phase).

They had also established briefing groups. The senior management team was meeting monthly to clarify their intentions and the purpose of actions amongst themselves. Moreover, they were having quarterly briefing meetings with middle management to insure the purpose of action was made known to the rest of the company.

Low evaluating and anticipating
The team had followed through in several ways to compensate for these weaknesses.

For example, the production director and the editorial director had been appointed to lead a project group which was surveying future products of the company. The production director had been appointed partly for his high anticipating (26 per cent) and the editorial director for his moderate evaluating (12 per cent — the highest in the team). The Action Profiling study had made it apparent that both of these men "scanned" the environment and that the production man in particular was in touch with long-range issues.

The managing director felt Action Profiling helped the team group people together to make more use of individual strengths. In this particular instance, prior to the team study, the marketing director would probably have been appointed to head the project group. He was low in evaluating and anticipating and, recognising this, he was able to be less protective of his territory because of understanding gained from the team study.

More generally, the team felt they were beginning to clarify issues about their product mix and about the mission of the company (evaluating). The team felt they had improved their ability to think strategically (anticipating) and that they were better able to respond actively to the changing business environment than had been the case previously.

They felt they had not yet mastered the techniques of strategy implementation (training in this had been suggested by the Profiler), but they felt they were closer to "owning" this tool. The strategic data had been brought down to operating levels in the editorial department and in sales. (Interestingly, these two areas were headed respectively by the team evaluator and the team anticipator.) The team also felt that they had not succeeded in quantifying objectives, although they were working on it and had been able to establish some yardsticks with which to measure change.

Emphasis on attending interaction
The team had capitalised on its strong attention-sharing interaction and had established working lunches.

General effects of the team study
Team members felt they had a much greater understanding and recognition of the dominant aspects of each other's working styles. As a result the dominant aspects of style had ceased to be an irritation to each other.

Team members found themselves using some Action Profiling labels about each other. They found these accurate and not misleading, although oversimplified.

The managing director felt that people were taking responsibility for the group process, intervening and drawing each other's attention to an individual who was making a needed contribution.

And as for the overall success of the team building assignment? The managing director now feels he can have a discussion with his board. Clarity about the company mission and the ability to plan strategically have been improved. When the team makes a decision now, it is owned and committed to by everyone.

CHAPTER 14

Conclusion: A Personal Note

We have seen in the previous chapter how Action Profiling can be used to help senior teams cope better with the balancing act of making high-level decisions. Now for a personal note.

I have been trained by Warren Lamb and Pamela Ramsden to make Action Profiles. I make Profiles myself, train other people to make Profiles and use the concepts both formally and informally whenever I am working with other people.

I have found that Action Profiling has profoundly affected the way I deal with others. I believe that I have a tendency, which is not uncommon, to feel that the person whose decision-making process is different from mine is wrong, i.e. those who think as I think are right and those who think differently are wrong. When conflict arises in a meeting it often comes not from the content of the discussion but from the underlying methods and motives of those involved in the discussion.

For example, I was once involved in a meeting with a colleague who kept coming up with idea after idea and wanting to put all of them into action. I became increasingly annoyed since many of the ideas were impractical or unimportant and to instigate them, in my opinion, would have been wasted effort. Luckily I knew that this colleague's Profile was quite different from mine. Rather than just reacting negatively to all his suggestions, which was what I felt like doing, I slowed myself down and repeated to him, in slightly different words, what he was saying. In doing this, coupled with my knowledge of his Action Profile, I was able to understand his thought process.

He is an explorer with an awareness of timing. In this incident his underlying motivation could have been paraphrased like this: "Here are all these ideas and alternatives" (exploring). "Let's run them up a flagpole and see who salutes" (timing). "Then, if someone salutes, we'll figure out what to do" (more timing).

On the other hand, I am an evaluative explorer. I cannot begin to act on an idea, even to the extent of running it up a flagpole, until I have gauged whether or not it is important.

Once I grasped his thought process my annoyance evaporated. This did not mean that I was swept up in his go-getting enthusiasm for ideas that seemed unimportant to me. Rather I was able to recognise his contribution for *what it was*. I stopped being annoyed at *what it was not*. From this point onwards the meeting began to be productive.

The bedrock of Action Profiling is this. Each of us has a motivational profile which is uniquely characteristic. Understanding this concept and being able to articulate these characteristics as they occur has made me much more tolerant of other people. Now I see behaviour as the variegated flowering of people's needs and motivations. Sometimes my unique motivations are appropriate to the task at hand: sometimes a colleague's are more appropriate. Not only am I more tolerant of differences in behaviour but now I can also find ways to draw on a colleague's strengths. *Vive la difference!*

It is surprising how often I observe people getting into conflicts with each other because each person is secretly demanding that the other person be like him, i.e. think like him and make decisions like him. I often find that group discussions are not actually about the topic under consideration but are really a conflict between the motivational needs of the participants. The explorer proposes "Let's try something new," the determined person growls "Let's be careful before we throw away what we've got," while the anticipator wants to know how much progress has been made. All three people are discussing the same topic. All three are making needed contributions in line with their innate characteristics and needs.

Probably the Action Profile is a kind of neuromuscular blueprint. It represents the energies that each of us has available for coping with the world. As we act in the world, like everything else in nature, we follow our blueprint. If we are allowed to do so, and given esteem and recognition for doing so, we can find a degree of fulfilment.

Less idealistically, I believe that Action Profiling works by identifying and labelling certain kinds of behaviours. These designations help to legitimise behaviours, to make them acceptable and understandable in oneself and in others.

Certainly there are many other aspects of personality and behaviour of which we need to be made aware, but if the Action Profile helps us to understand ourselves better, to understand and accept others more fully and to work more productively and less divisively with one another — and this certainly has been my experience — then it is making a lasting contribution, within the workplace, outside it and wherever people must make decisions together.

Bibliography

Bartenieff, Irmgard, and Dori Lewis, *Body Movement: Coping with the Environment*, New York, Gordon and Breach, 1980.

Davis, Flora, *Inside Intuition: What We Know About Nonverbal Communication*, New York, The New American Library, 1973.

Davis, Martha, *Towards Understanding the Intrinsic in Body Movement*, New York, Arno Press, 1975.

Kestenberg, Judith S., et al., *Children and Parents: Psychoanalytic Studies in Development*, New York, Jason Aaronson, 1975.

Laban, Rudolf, *The Mastery of Movement*, 4th ed., Revised by Lisa Ullman, Plymouth, Macdonald & Evans, 1980.

Laban, Rudolf, *The Language of Movement: A Guidebook to Choreutics*, Annotated and edited by Lisa Ullmann, Plymouth, Macdonald & Evans, 1974.

Laban, Rudolf, and F.C. Lawrence, *Effort*, Plymouth, Macdonald & Evans, 1974.

Lamb, Warren, *Posture and Gesture*, London, Duckworth, 1965.

Lamb, Warren, and David Turner, *Management Behaviour*, London, Duckworth, 1969.

Lamb, Warren, and Elizabeth Watson, *Body Code: The Meaning in Movement*, London and Boston, Routledge & Kegan Paul, 1979.

Ramsden, Pamela, *Top Team Planning*, London, Prentice Hall/Associated Business Press, 1973.

Scott, Susan, *Behaviour Theories*, London, Coverdale Educational, 1975.

Index